Public Domain Vintage Picture Adult Coloring Book

Coloring Art Works from the Past

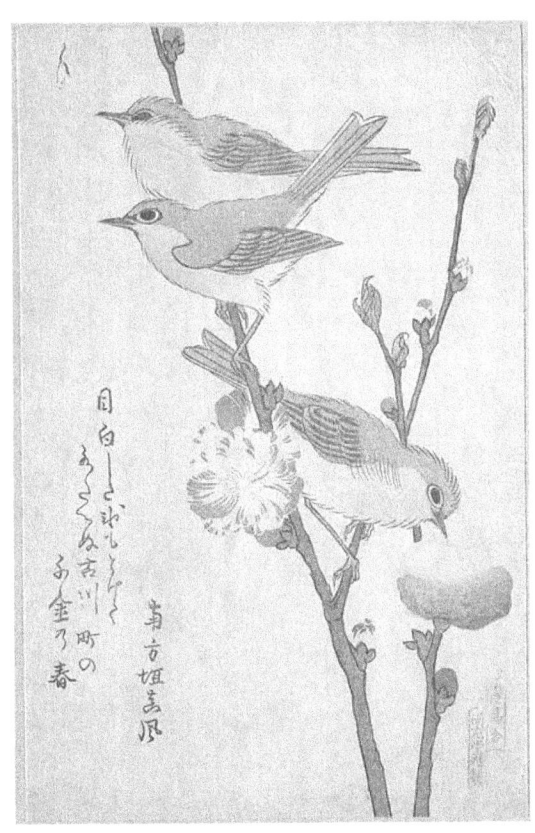

Public Domain Vintage Adult Coloring Book
Coloring art works from the past!

All Rights Reserved

© Loretta Emmons August 2018

Introduction

The artwork contained in this adult coloring book includes works of master artists dating back to the 1300's. These amazing works have been accumulated from all over the globe, where they have been restored for our enjoyment.

This coloring book is an enriching look at old works, from simple sketches to intricate architecture, and beautiful scenery.

As you color each page, and transcend the original artist's idea, enjoy experimenting with different mediums, color schemes to revitalize and in some cases perhaps complete an unfinished sketch.

Enjoy!

Dedicated to my family past and present. We have always been very interested in history and art. This adult coloring book is my foray into to past where art was meaningful, told a story, and was often disregarded.

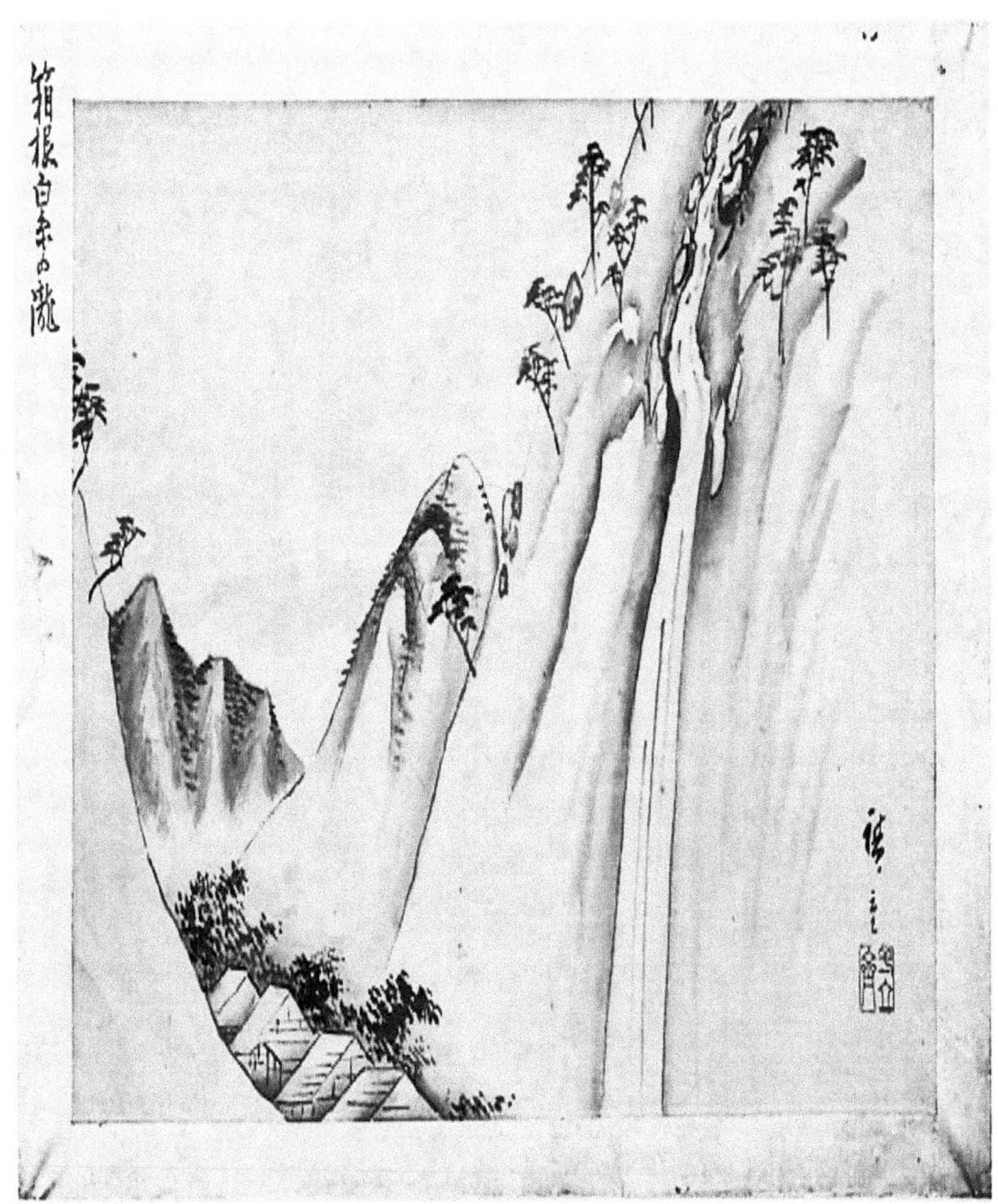

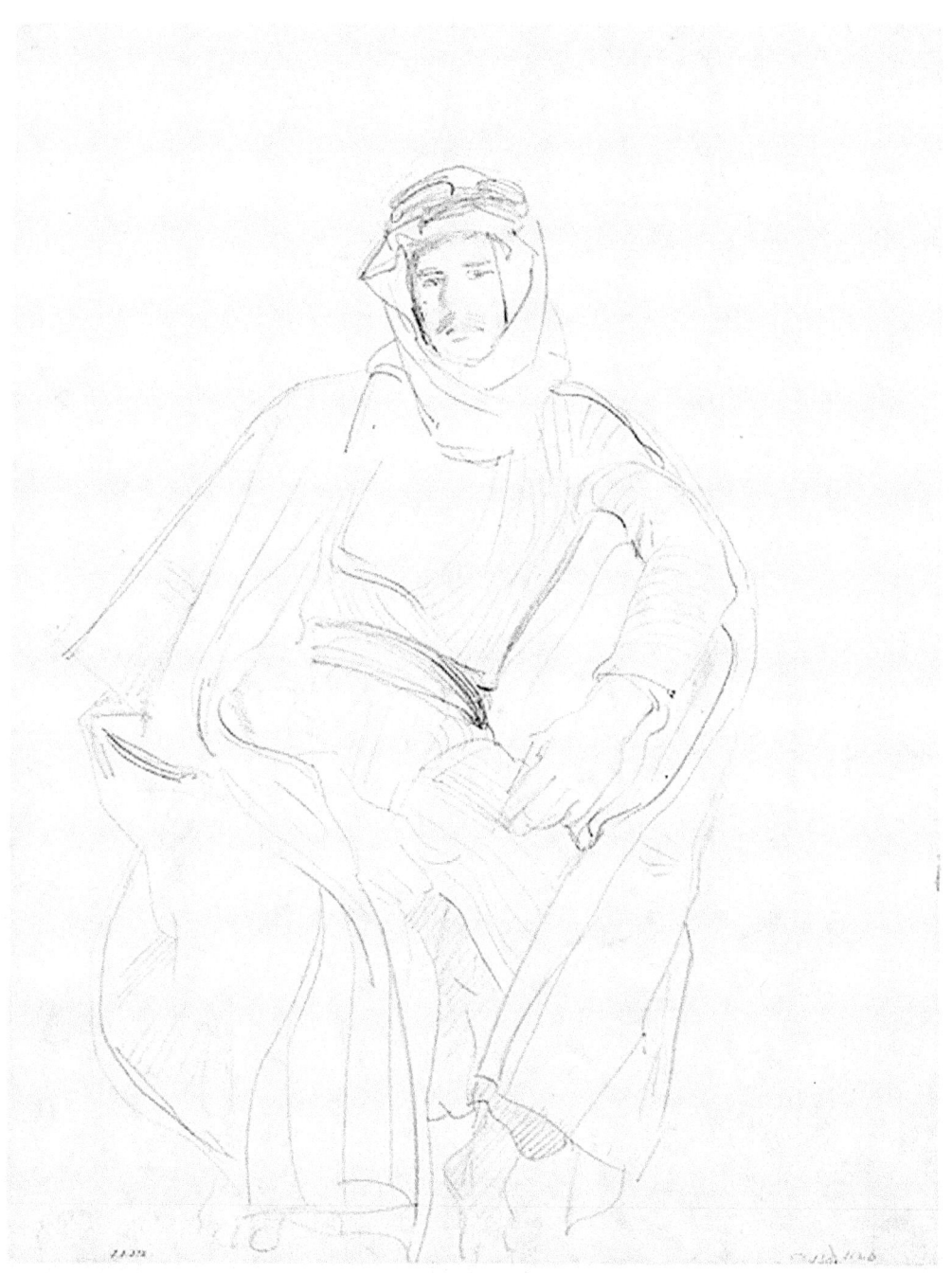

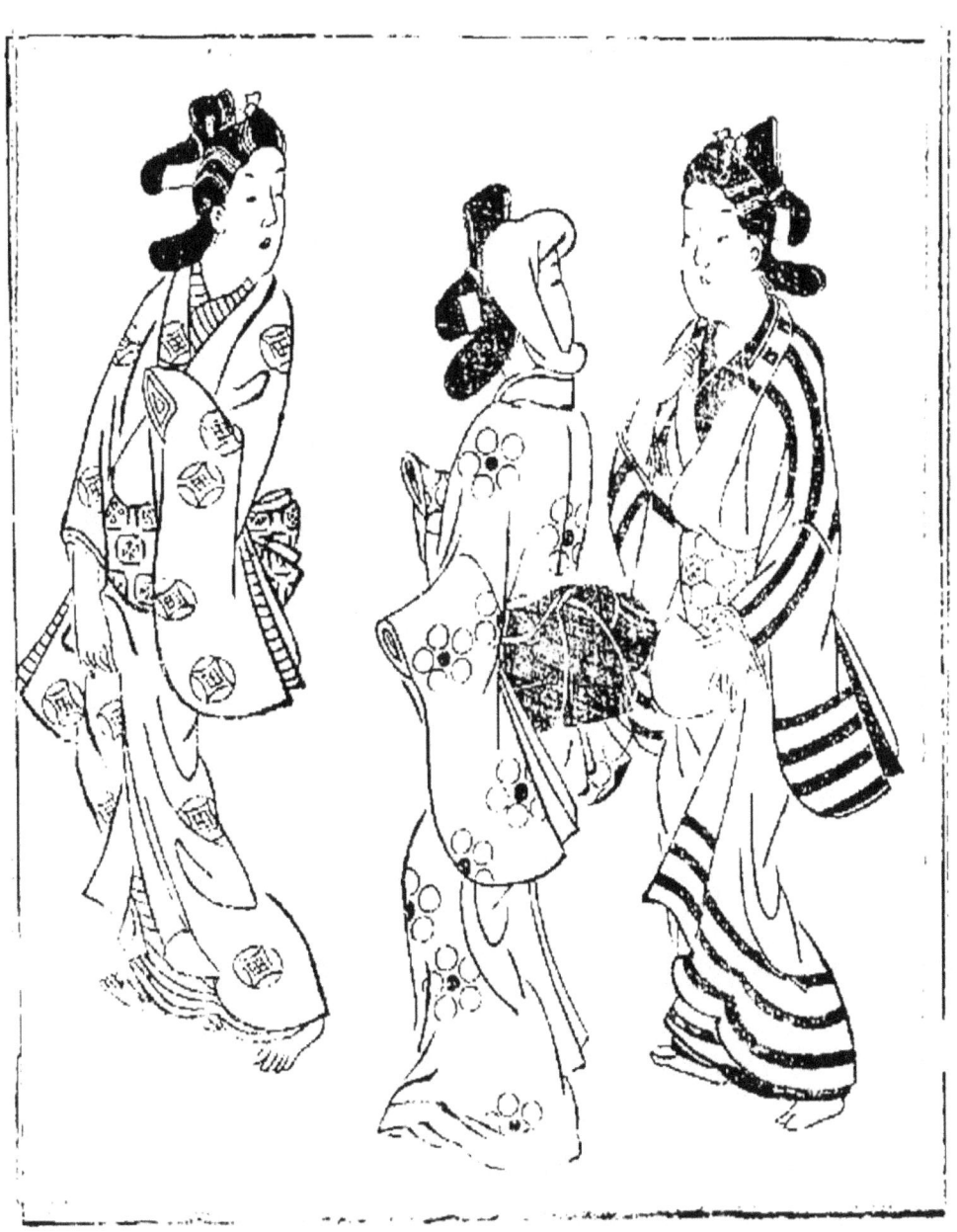

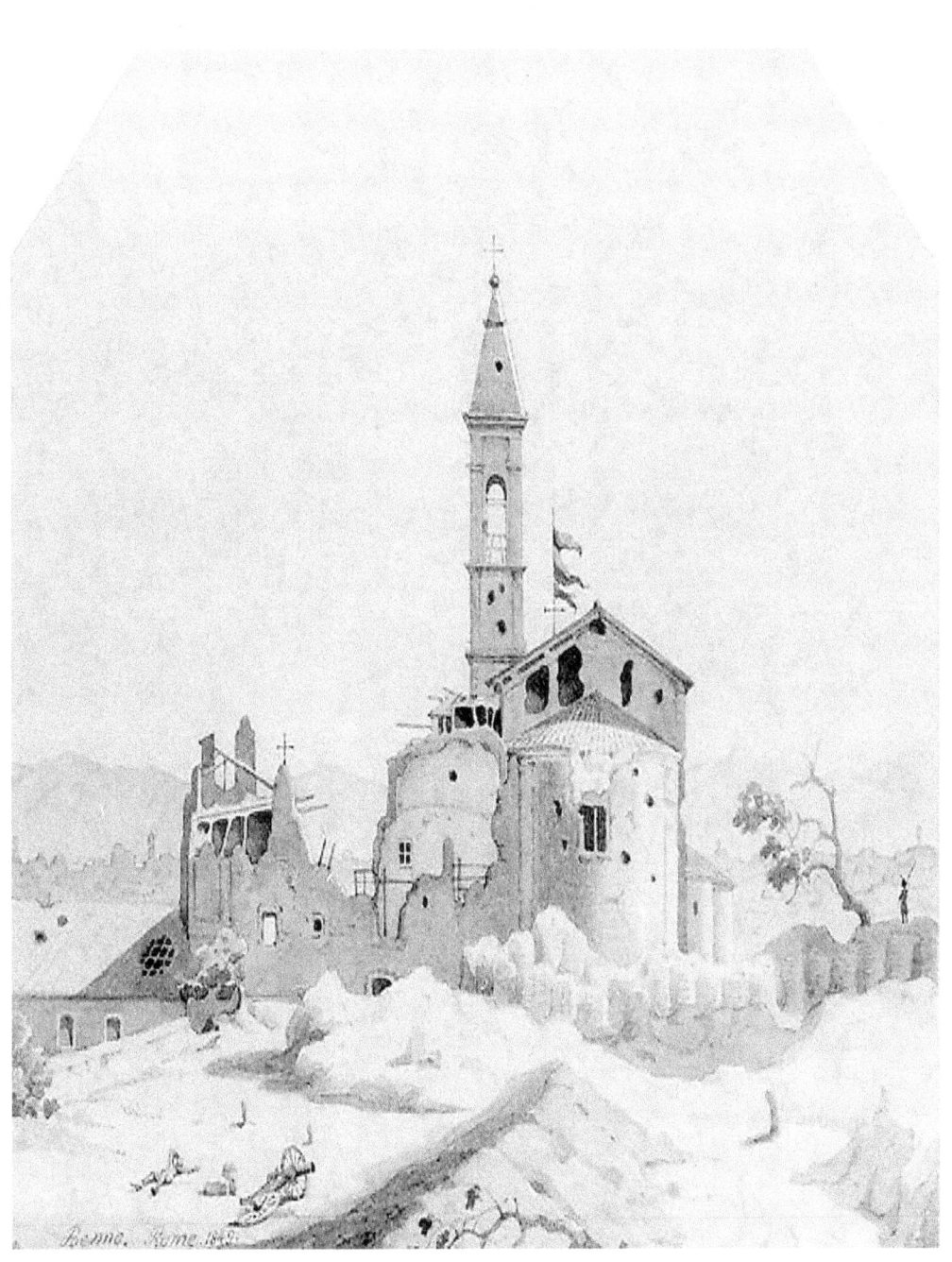

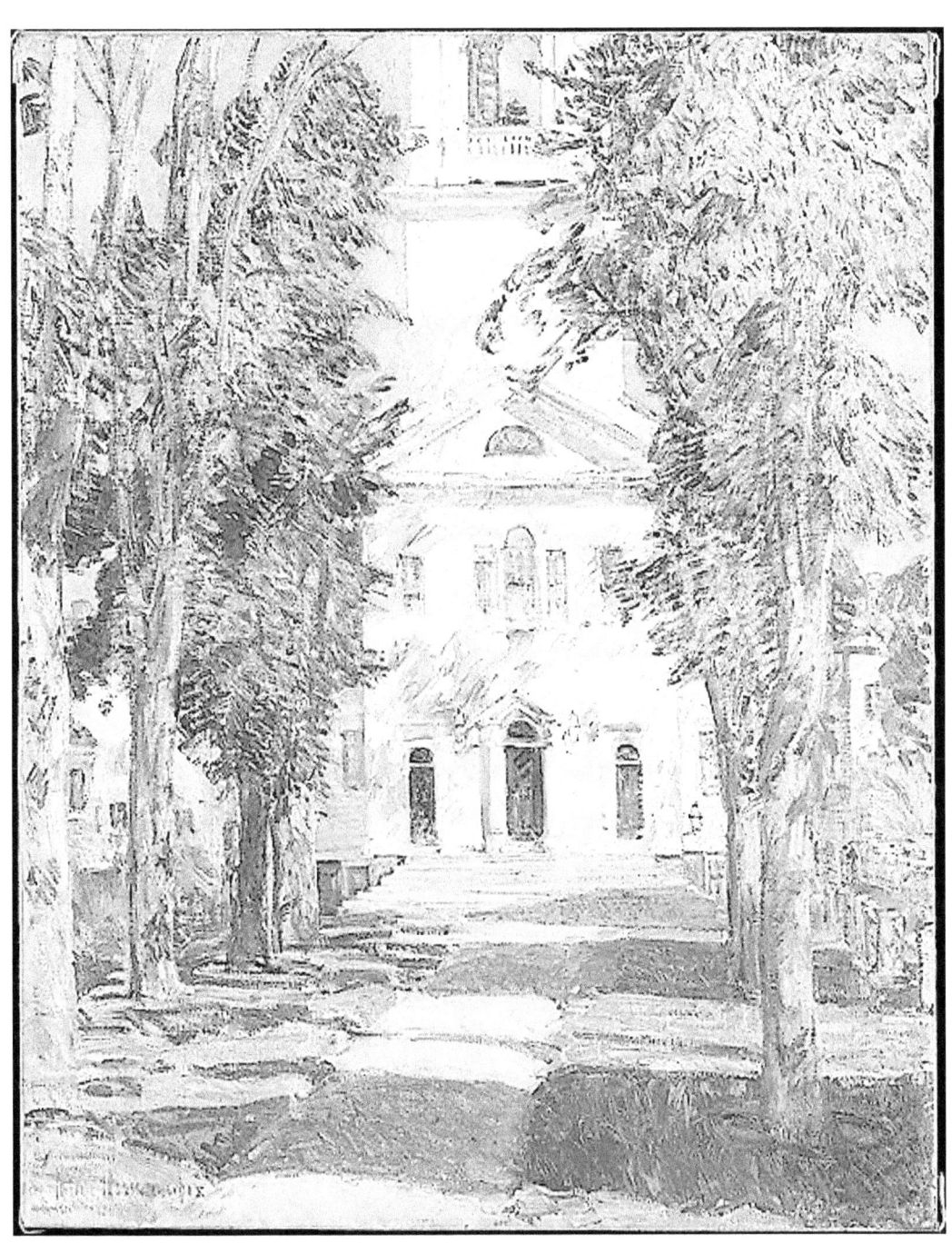

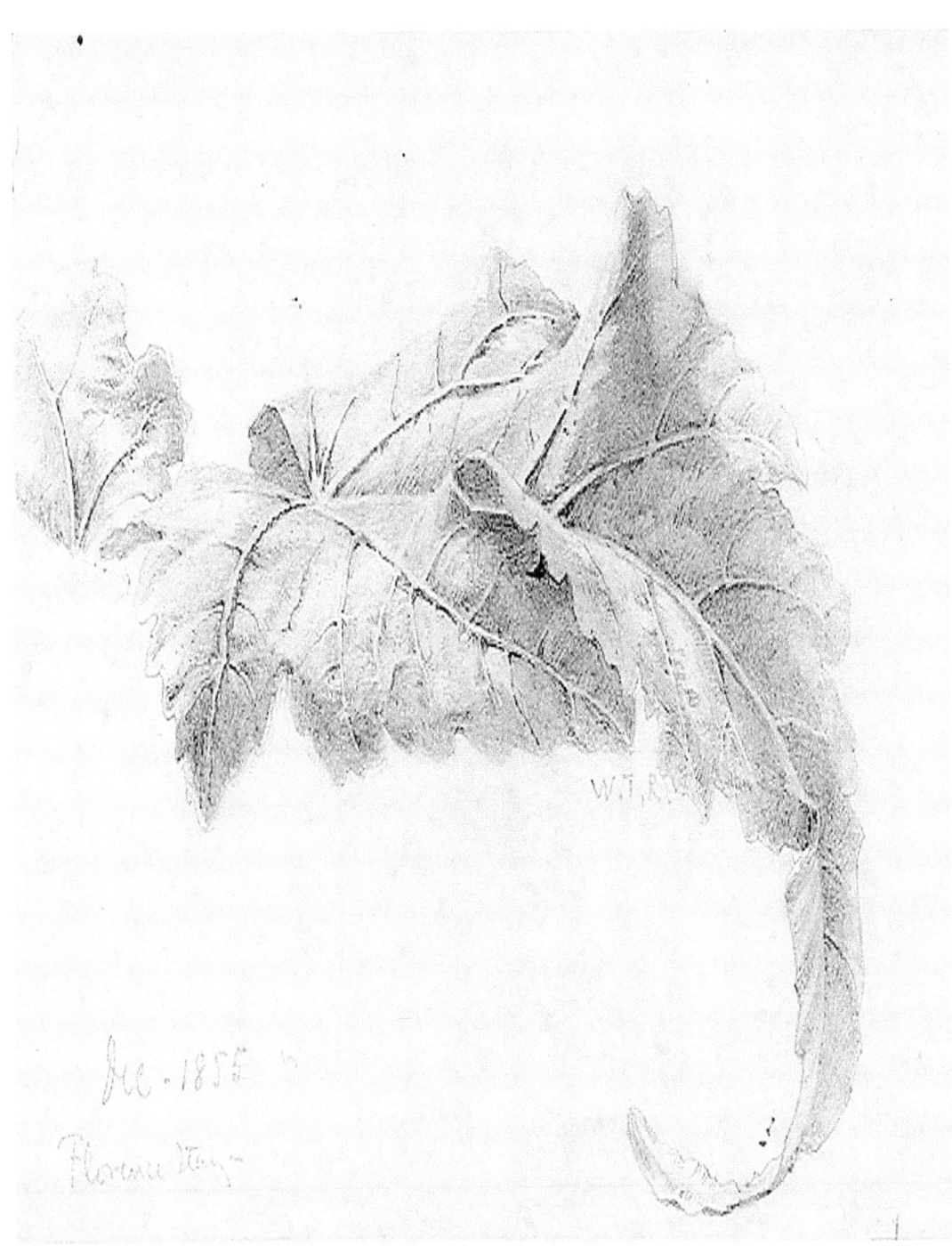

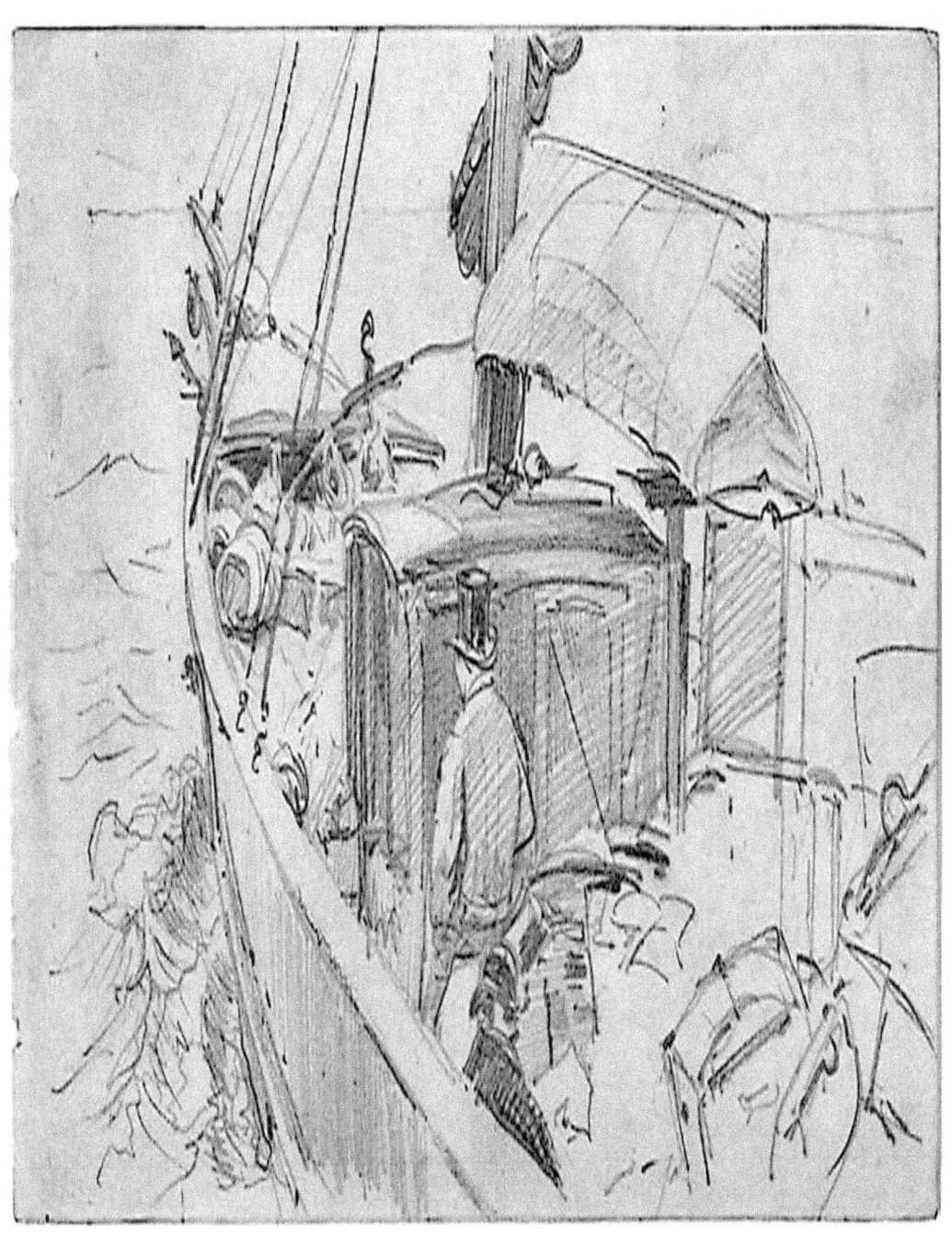

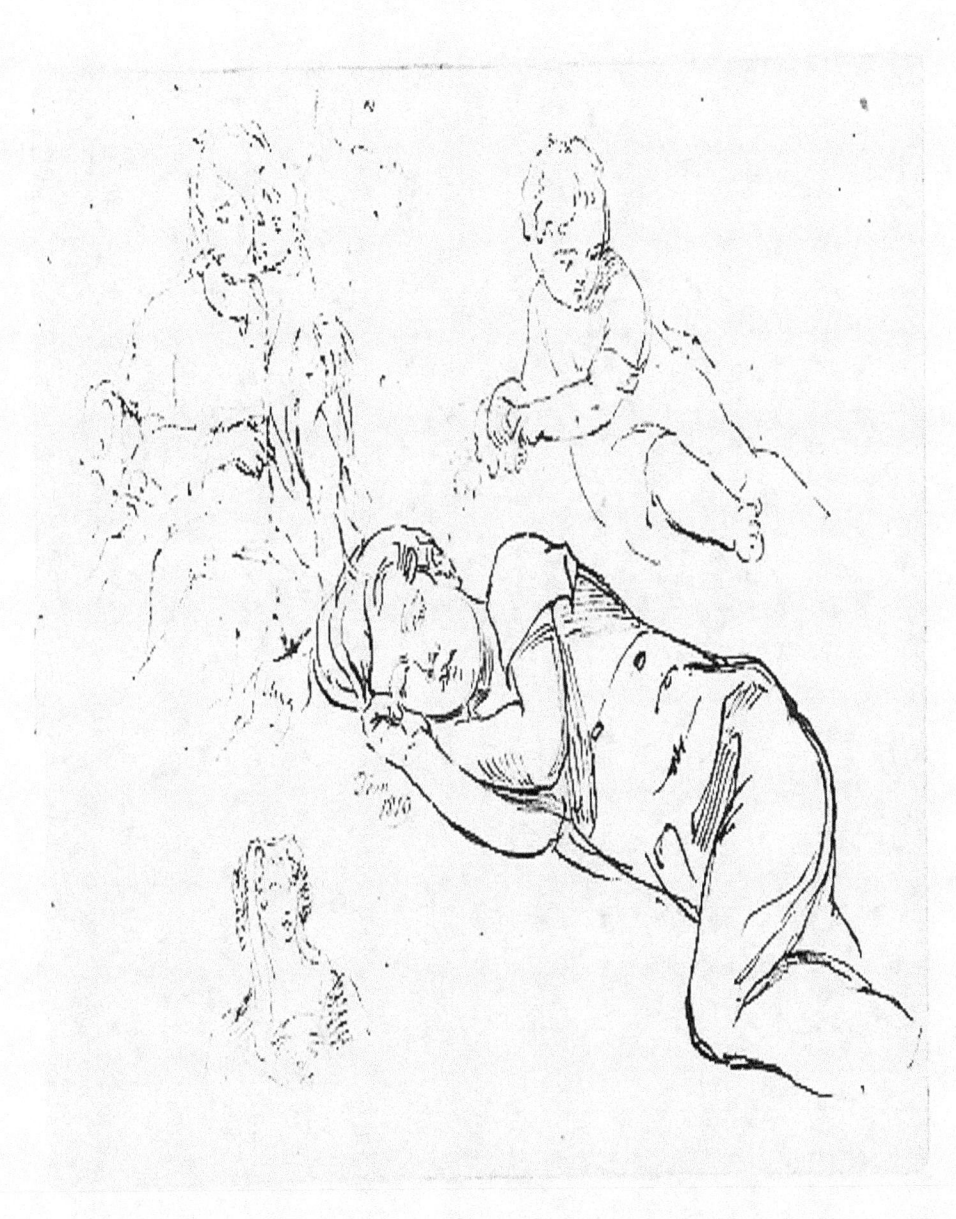

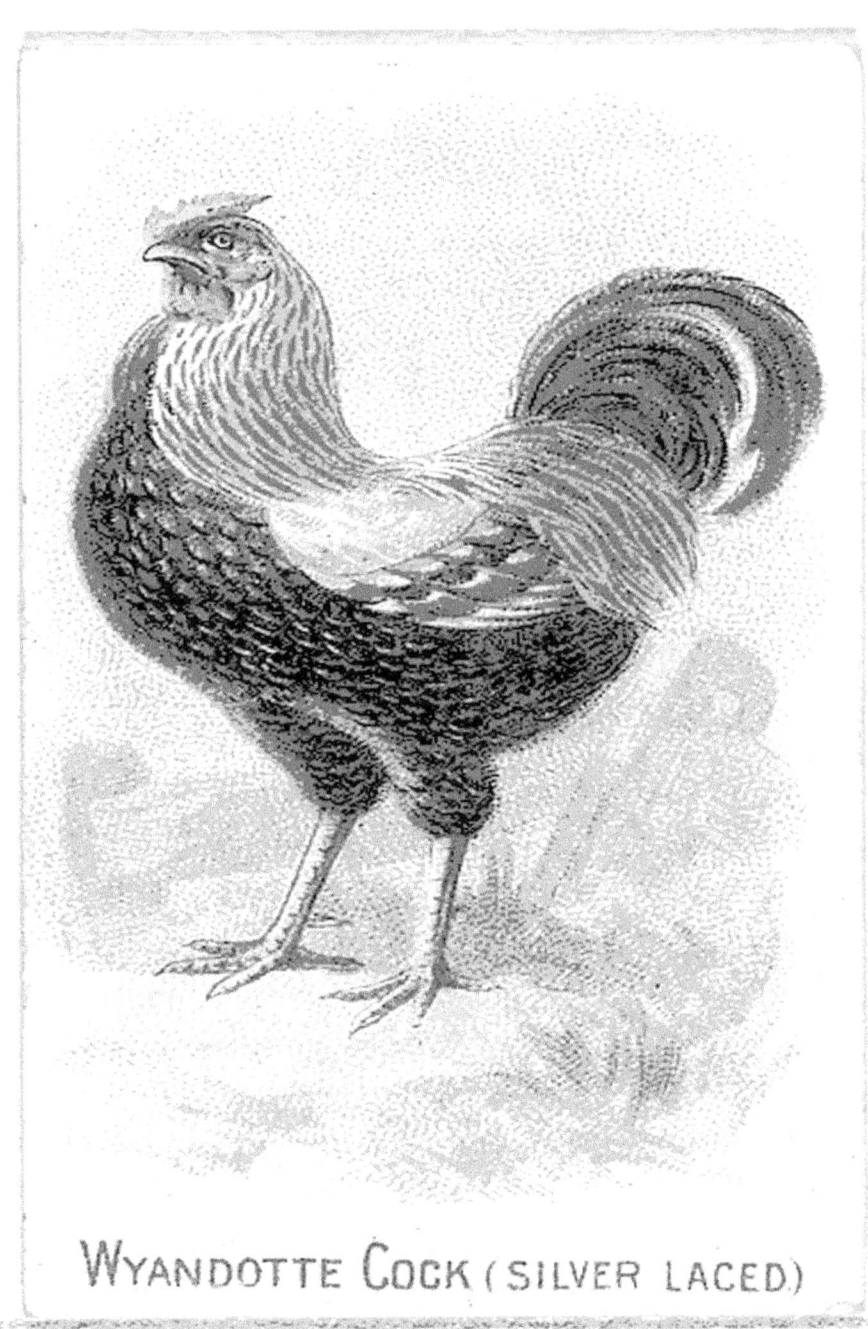

WYANDOTTE COCK (SILVER LACED.)

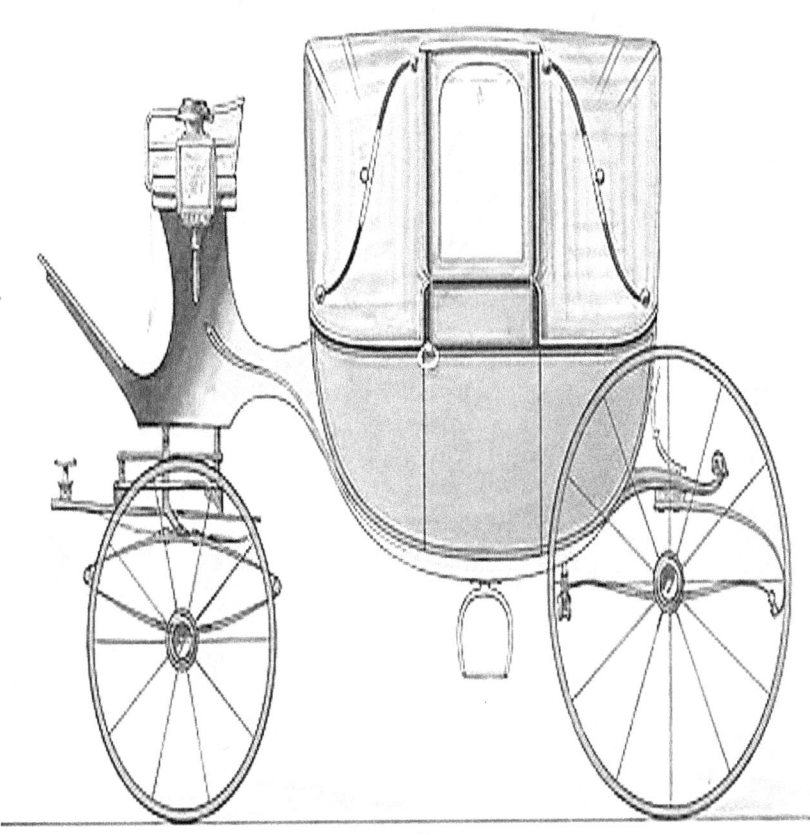

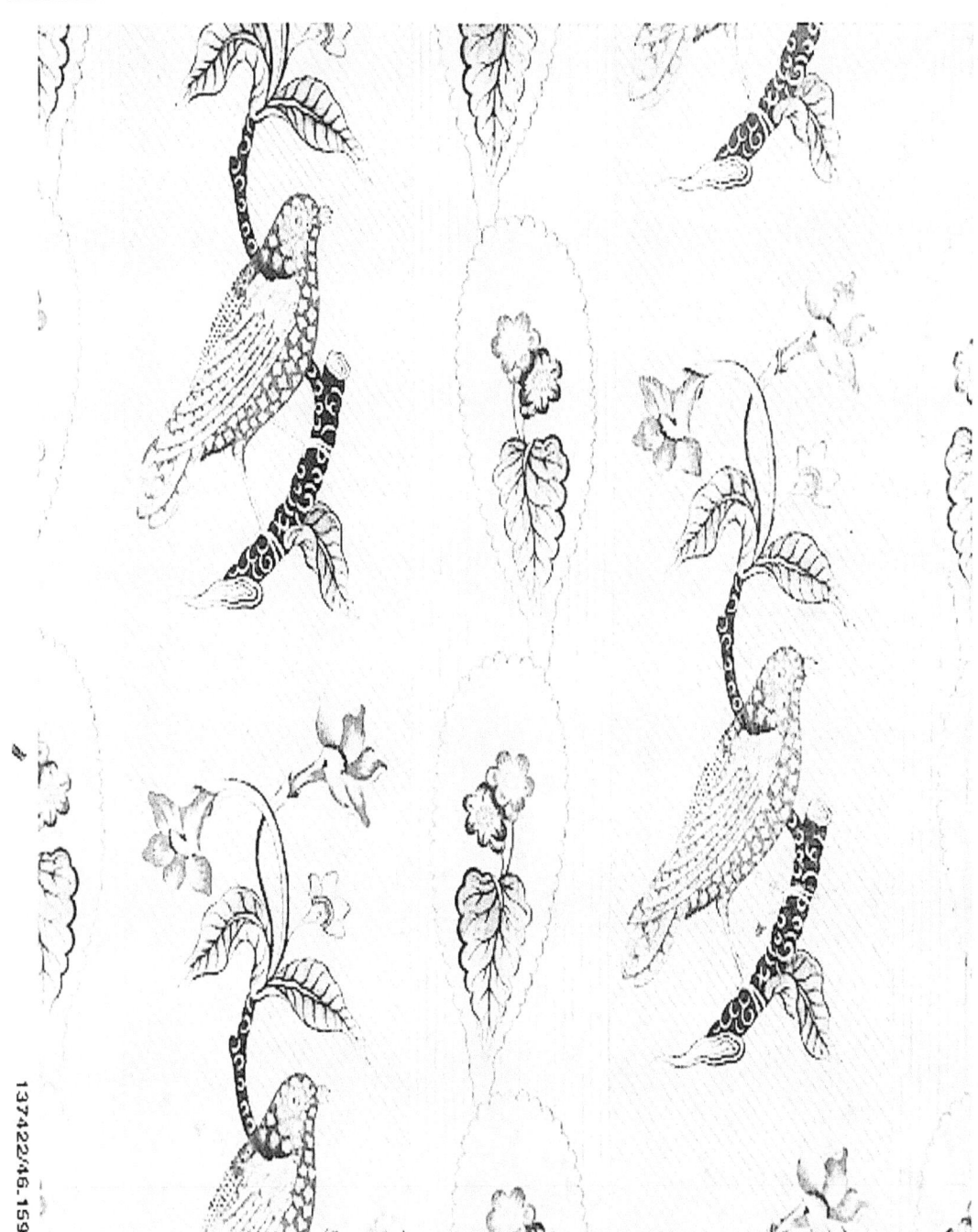

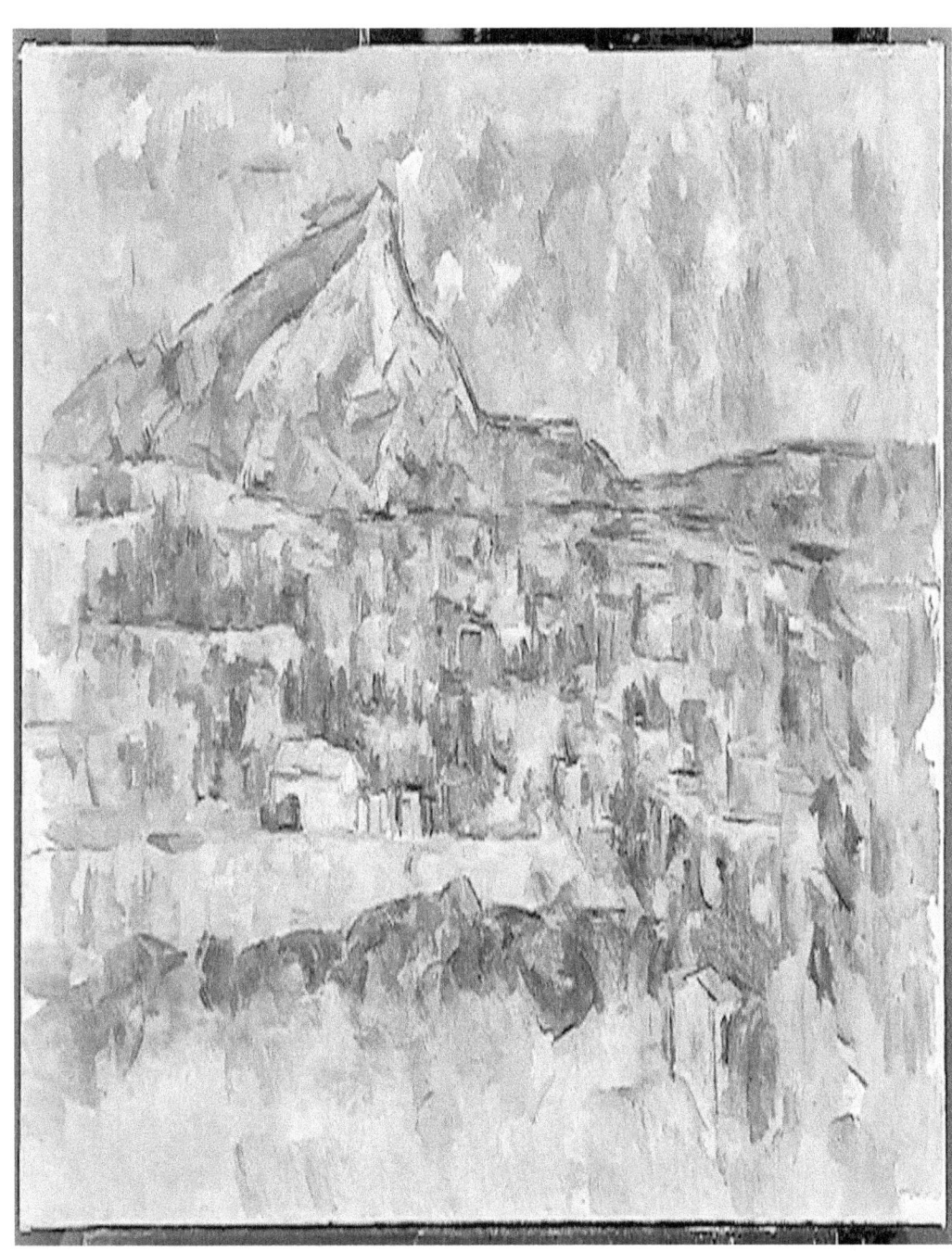

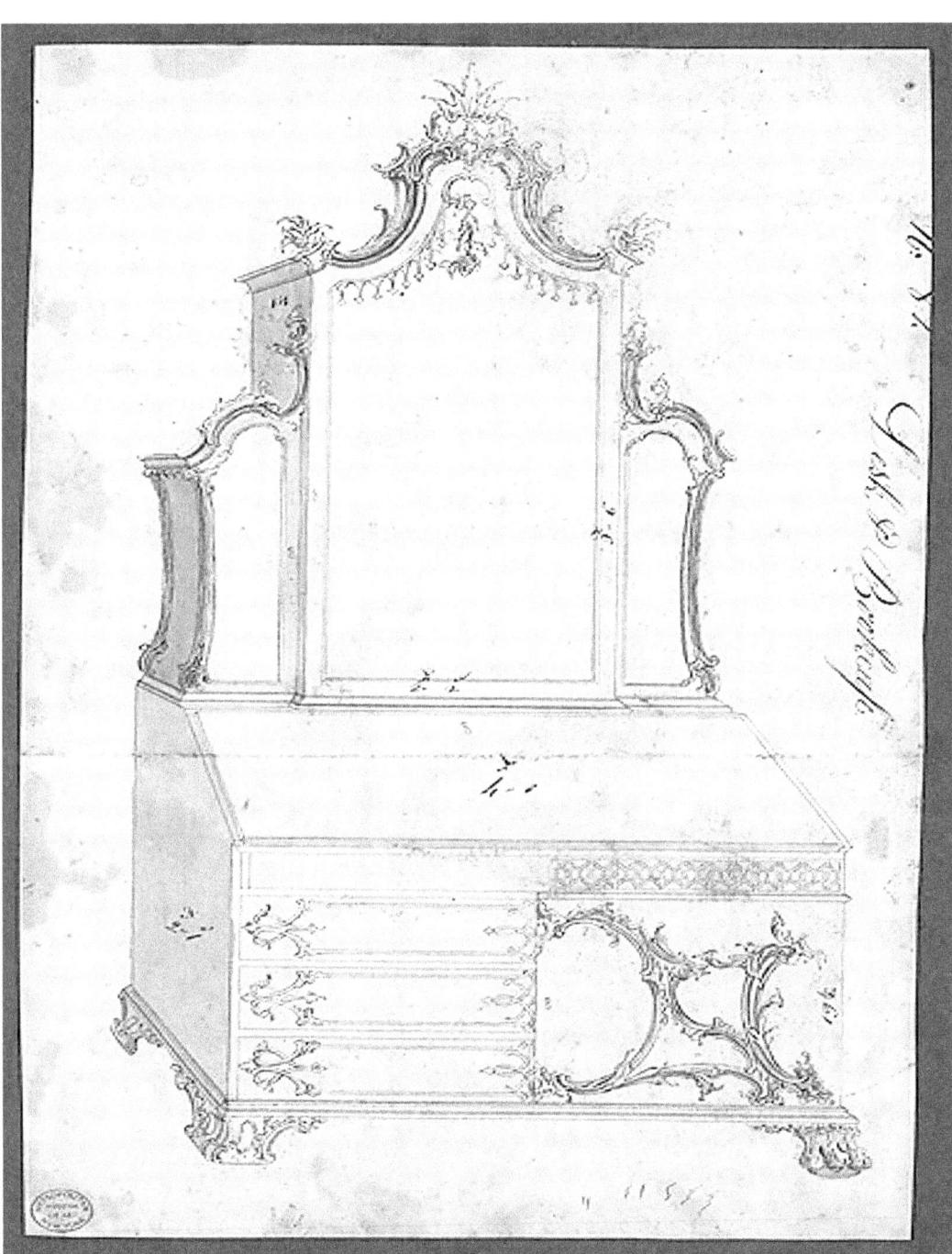

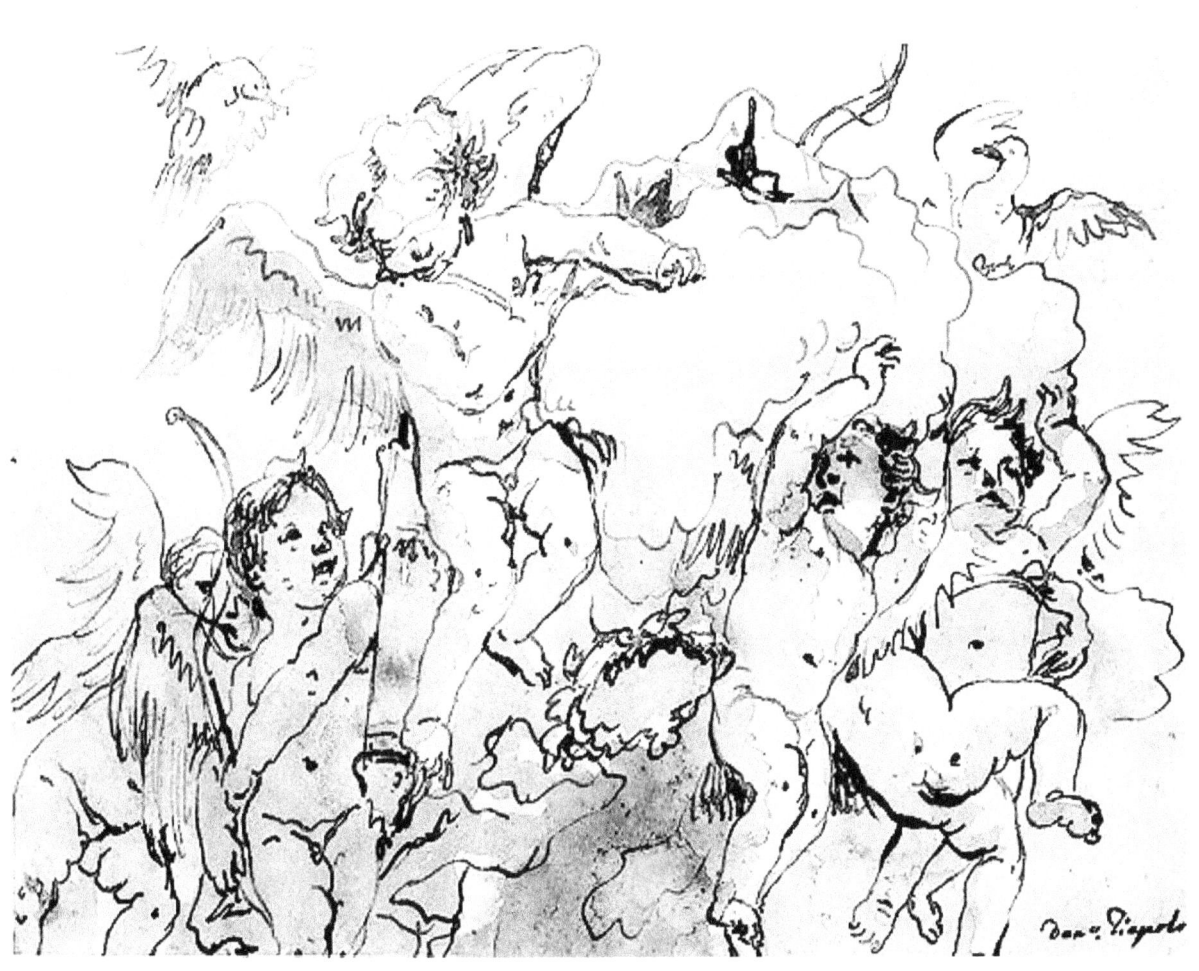

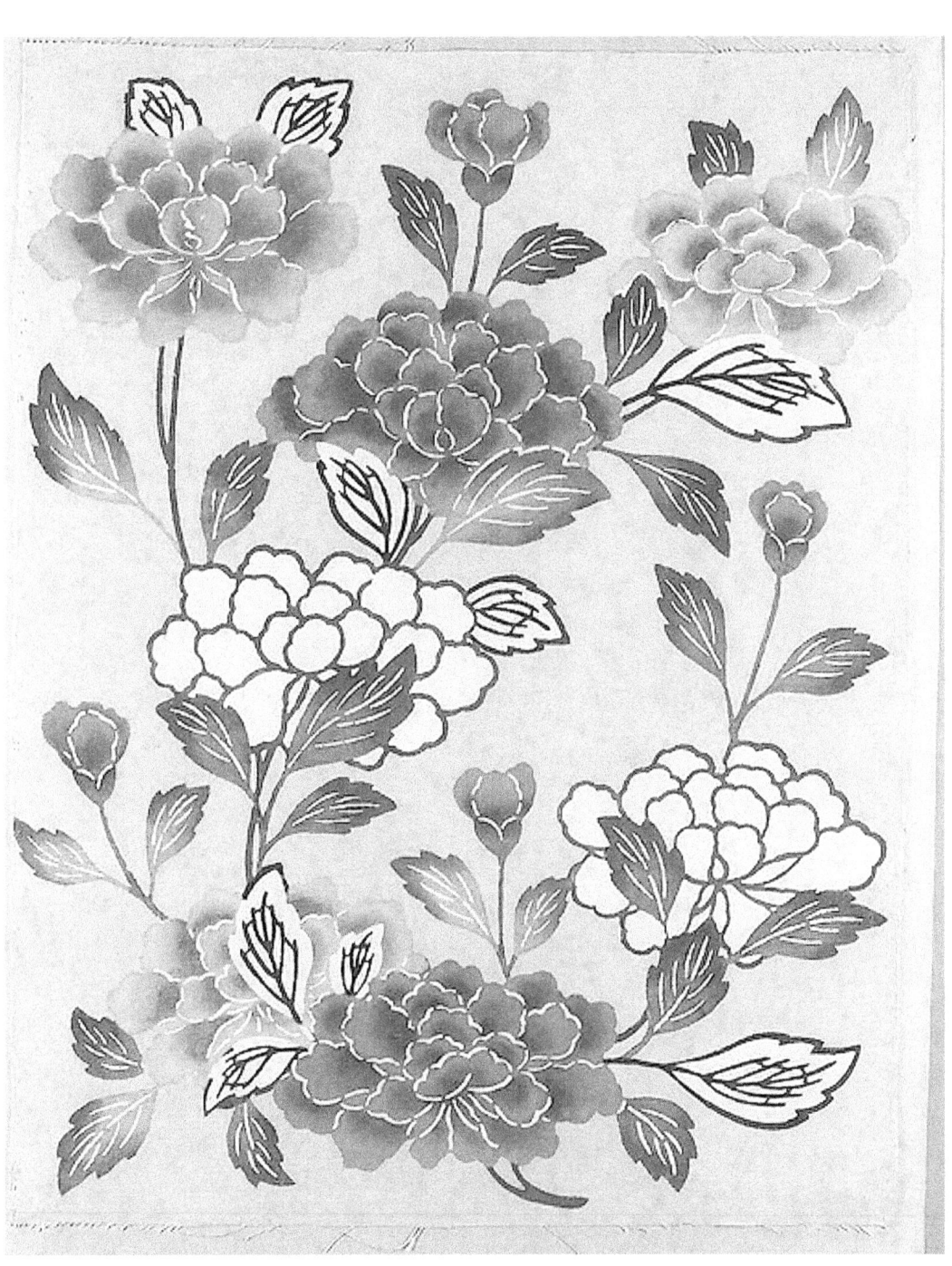

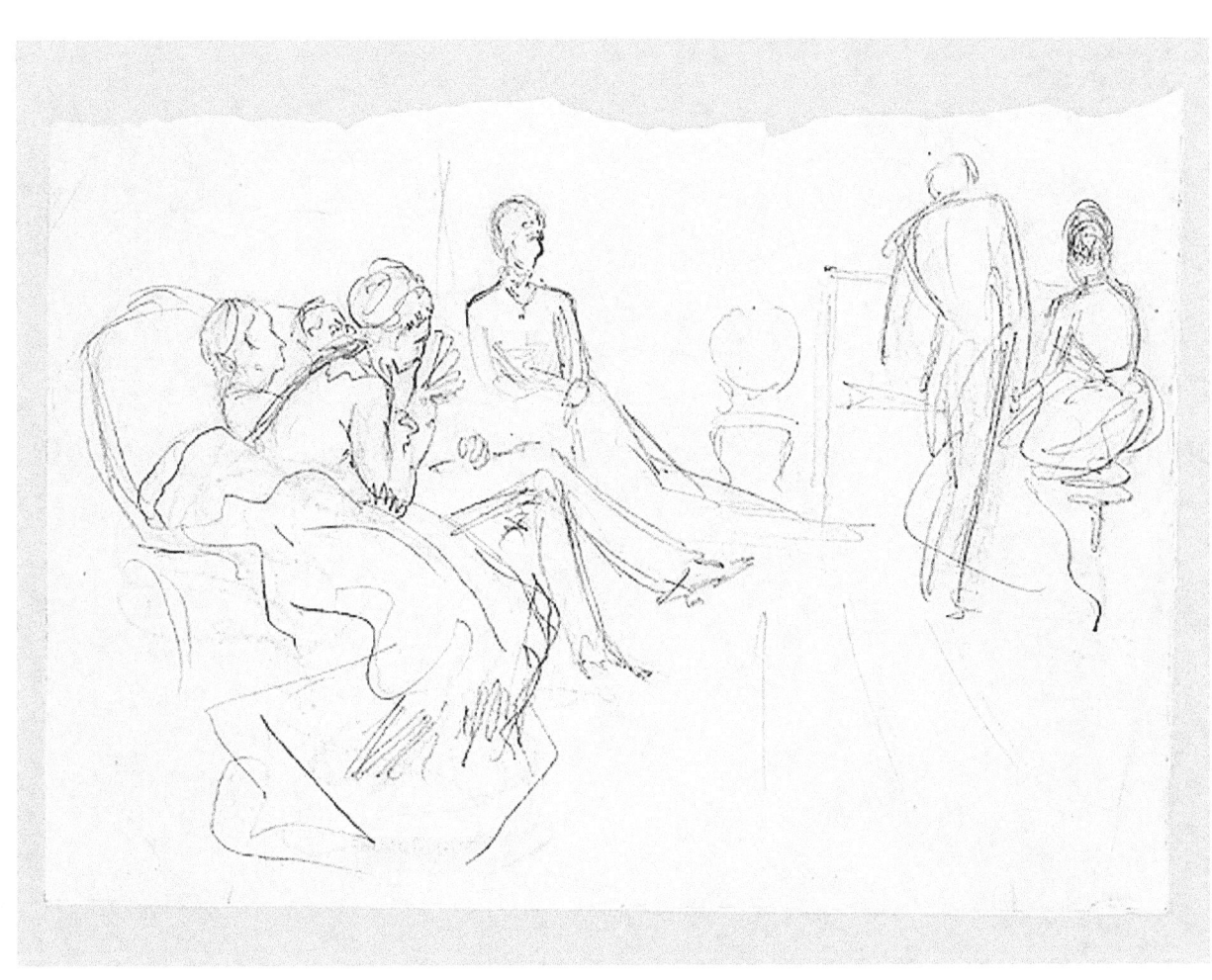

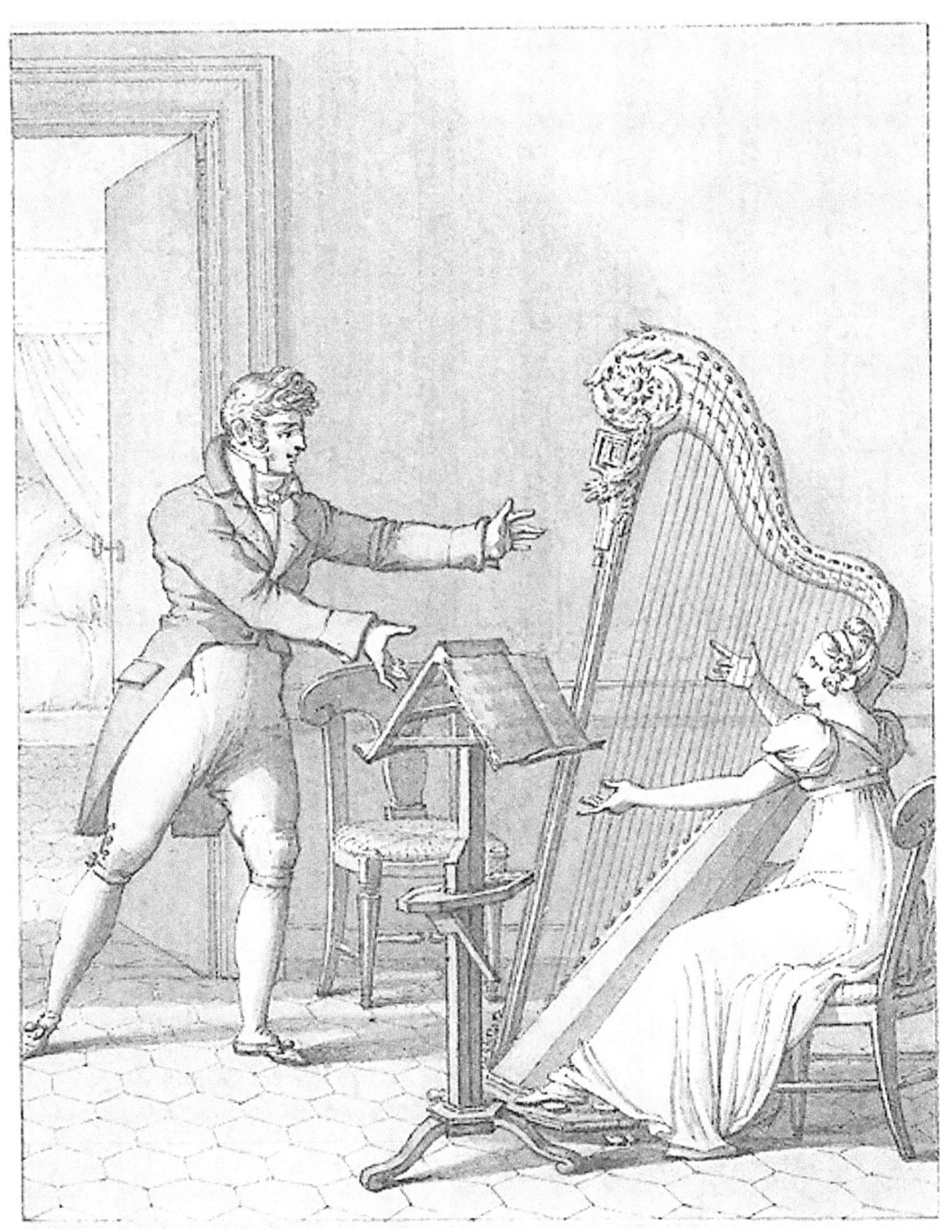

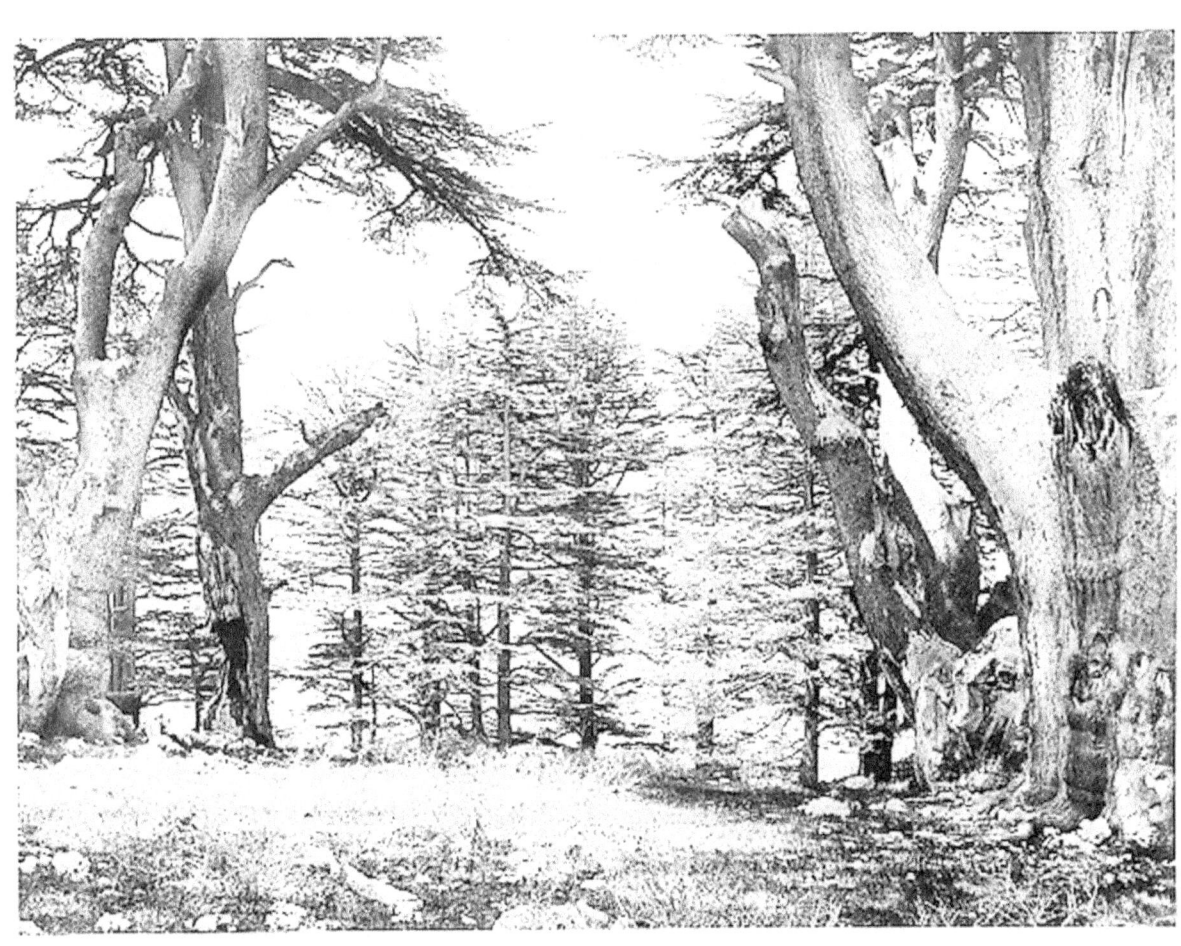

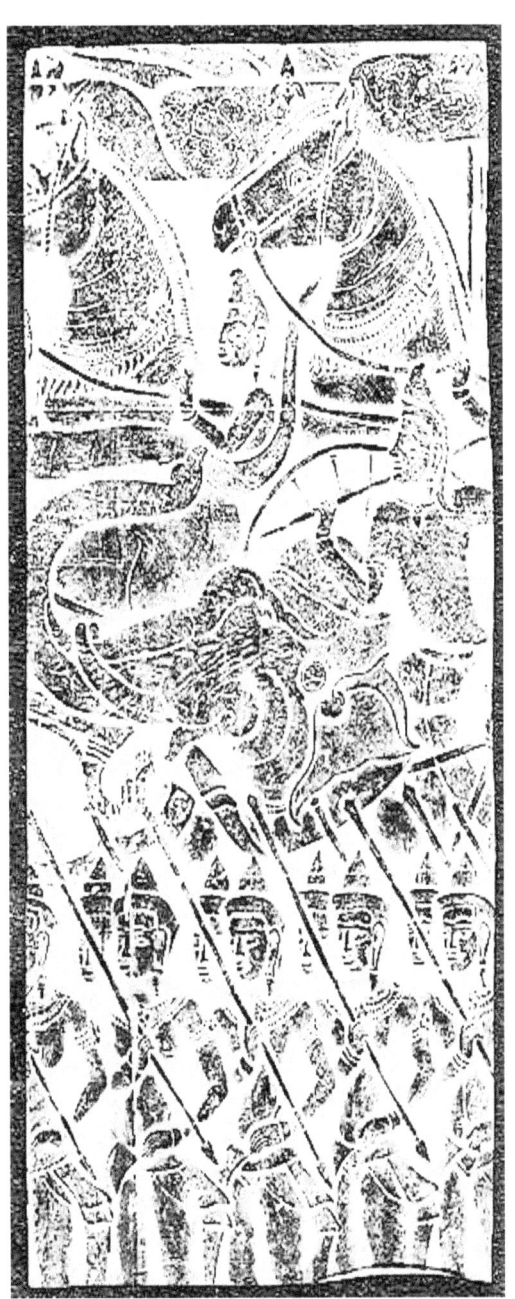

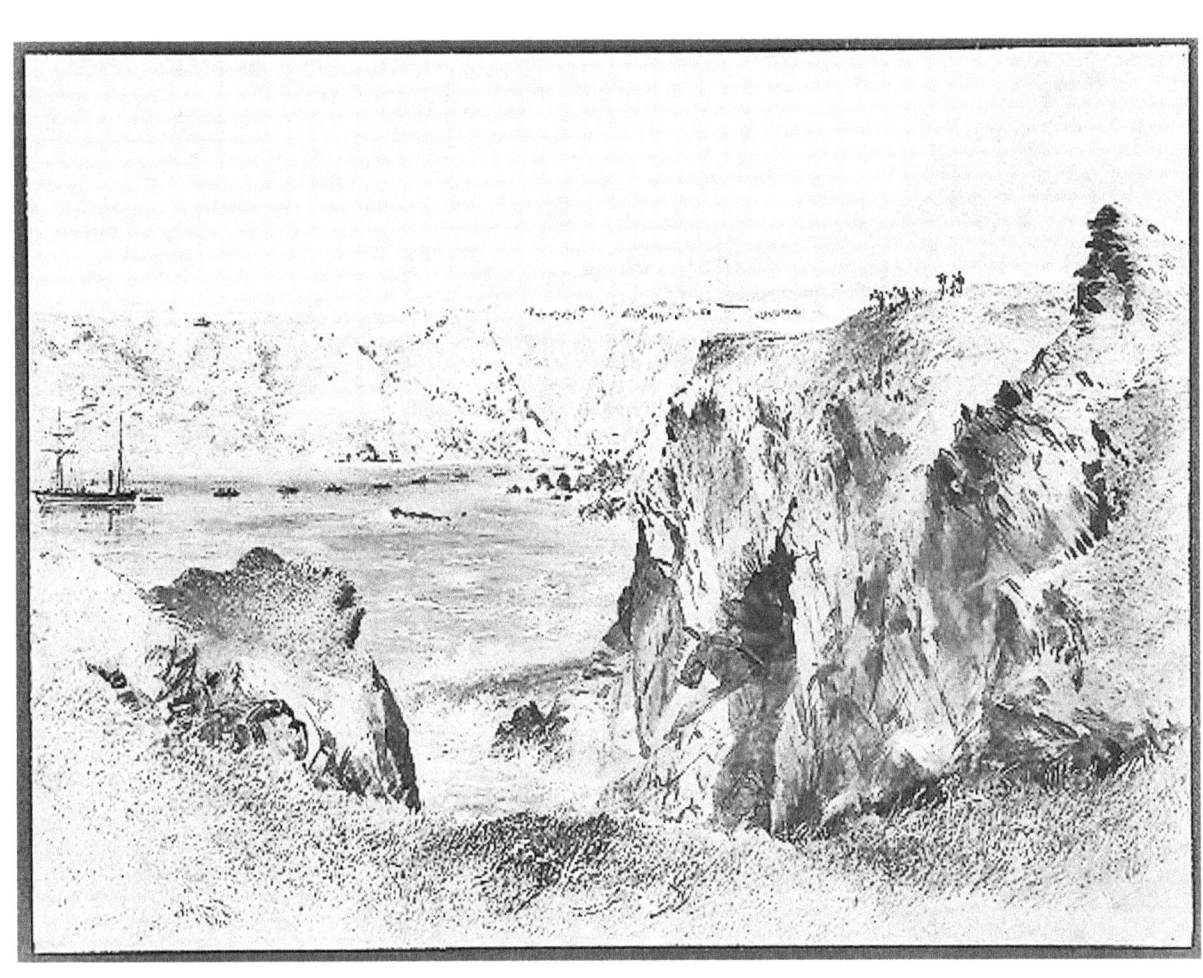

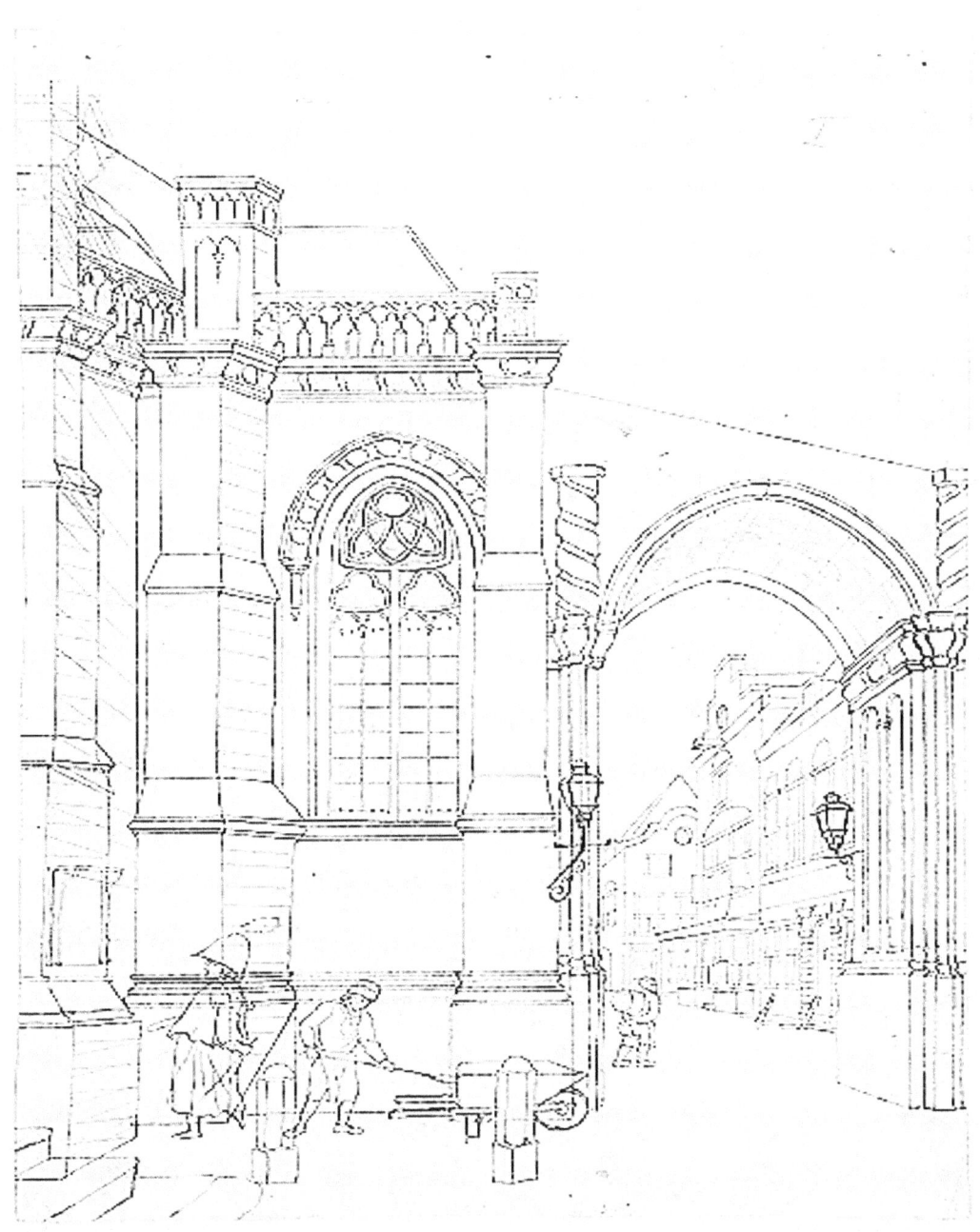

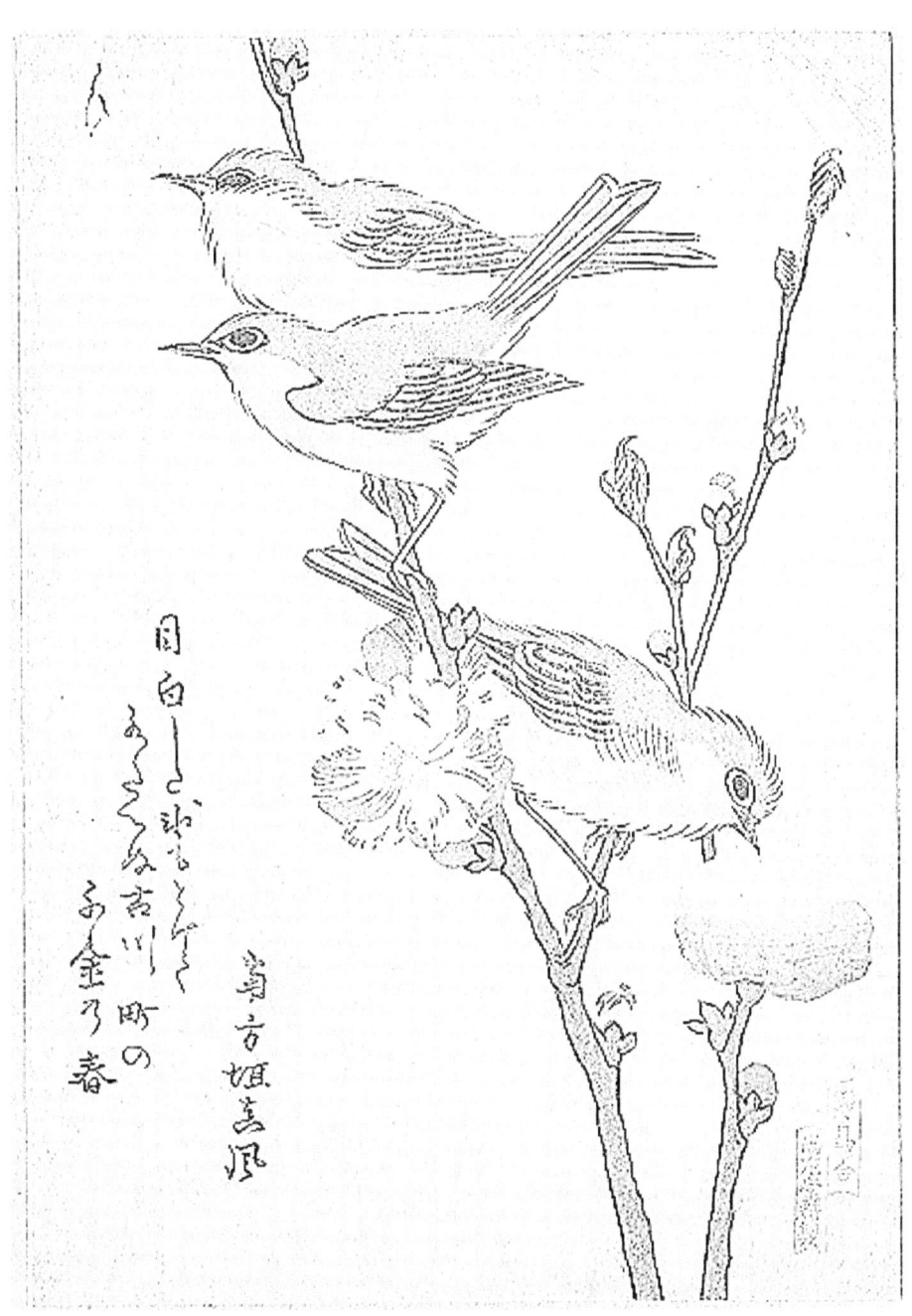

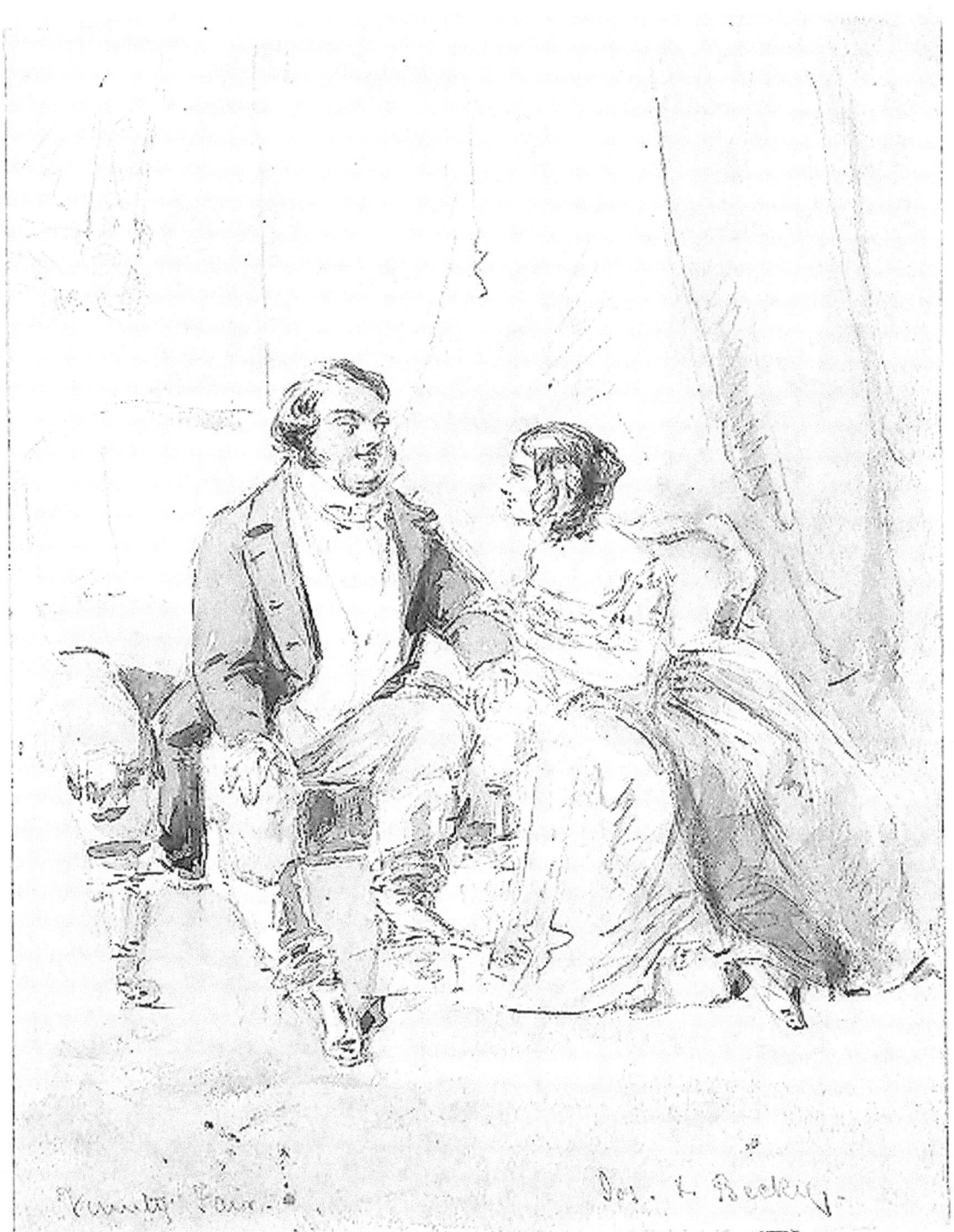

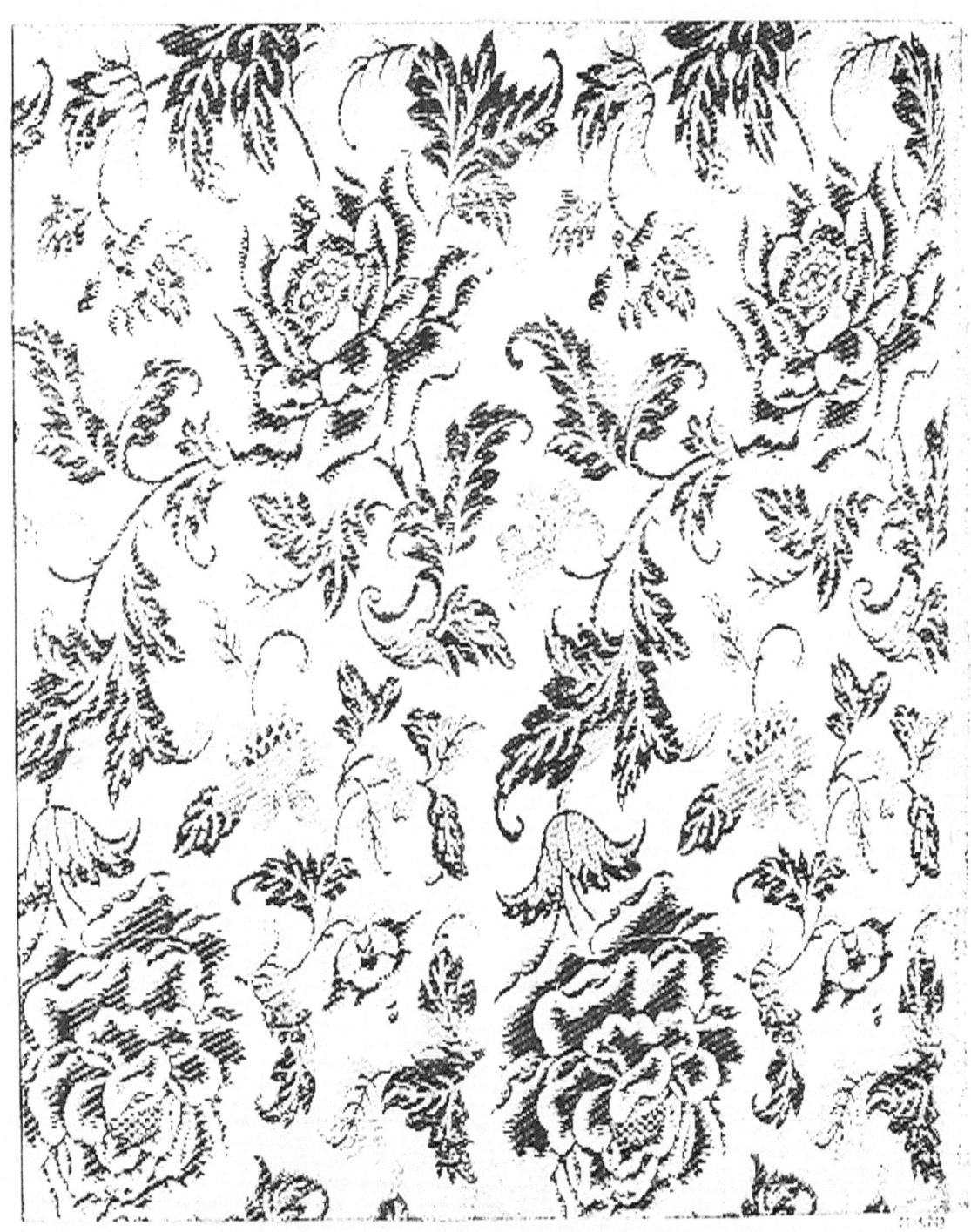

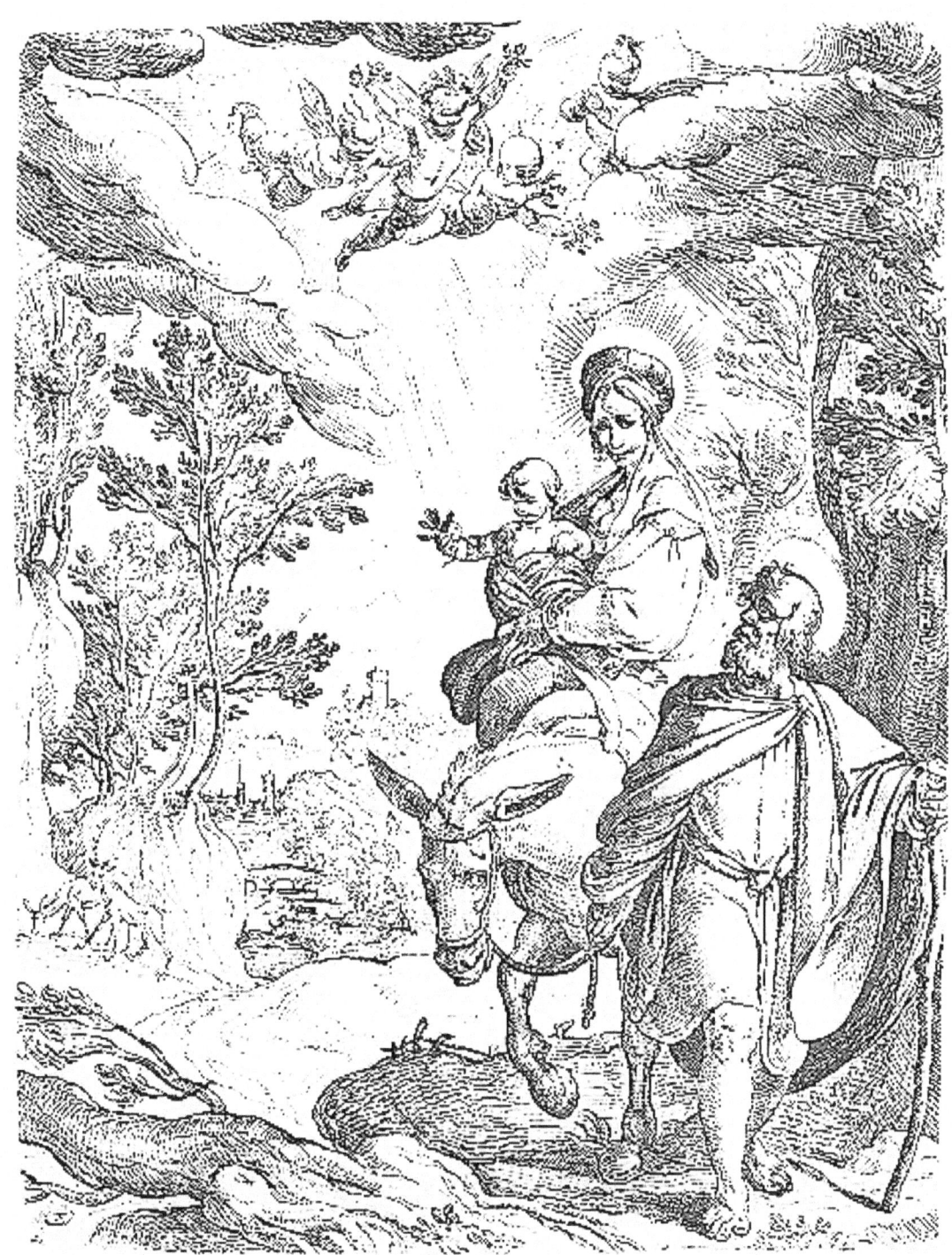

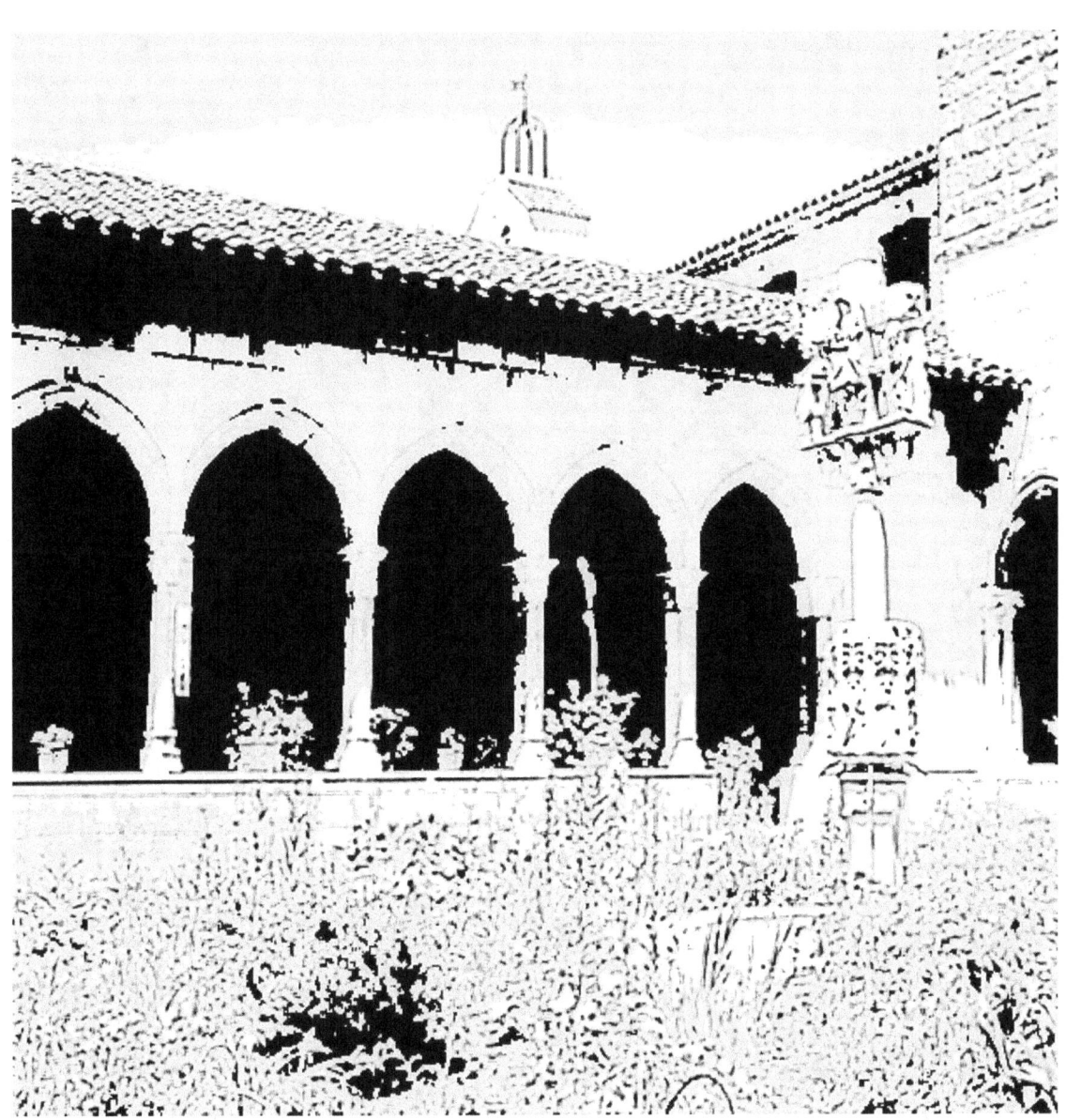

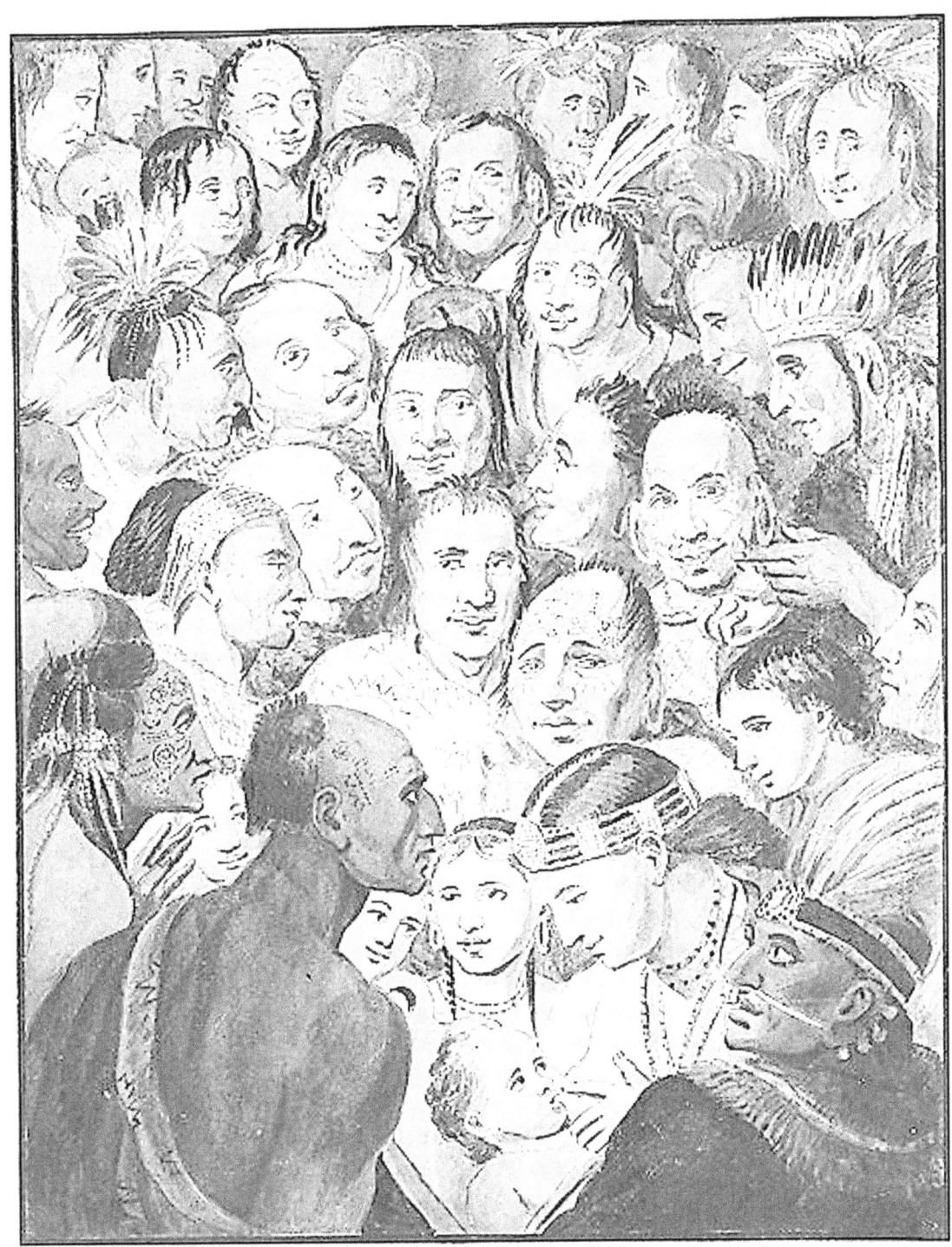

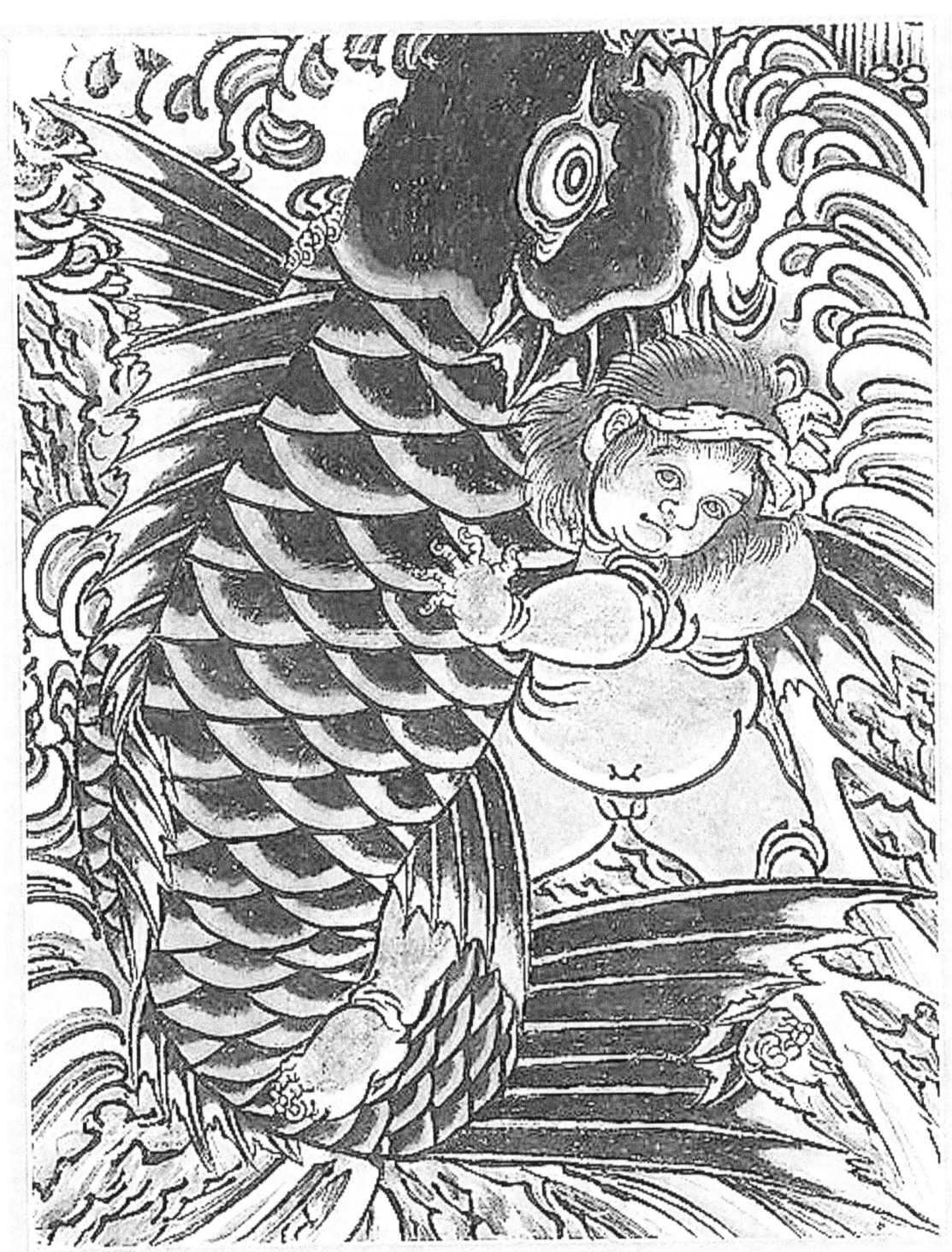

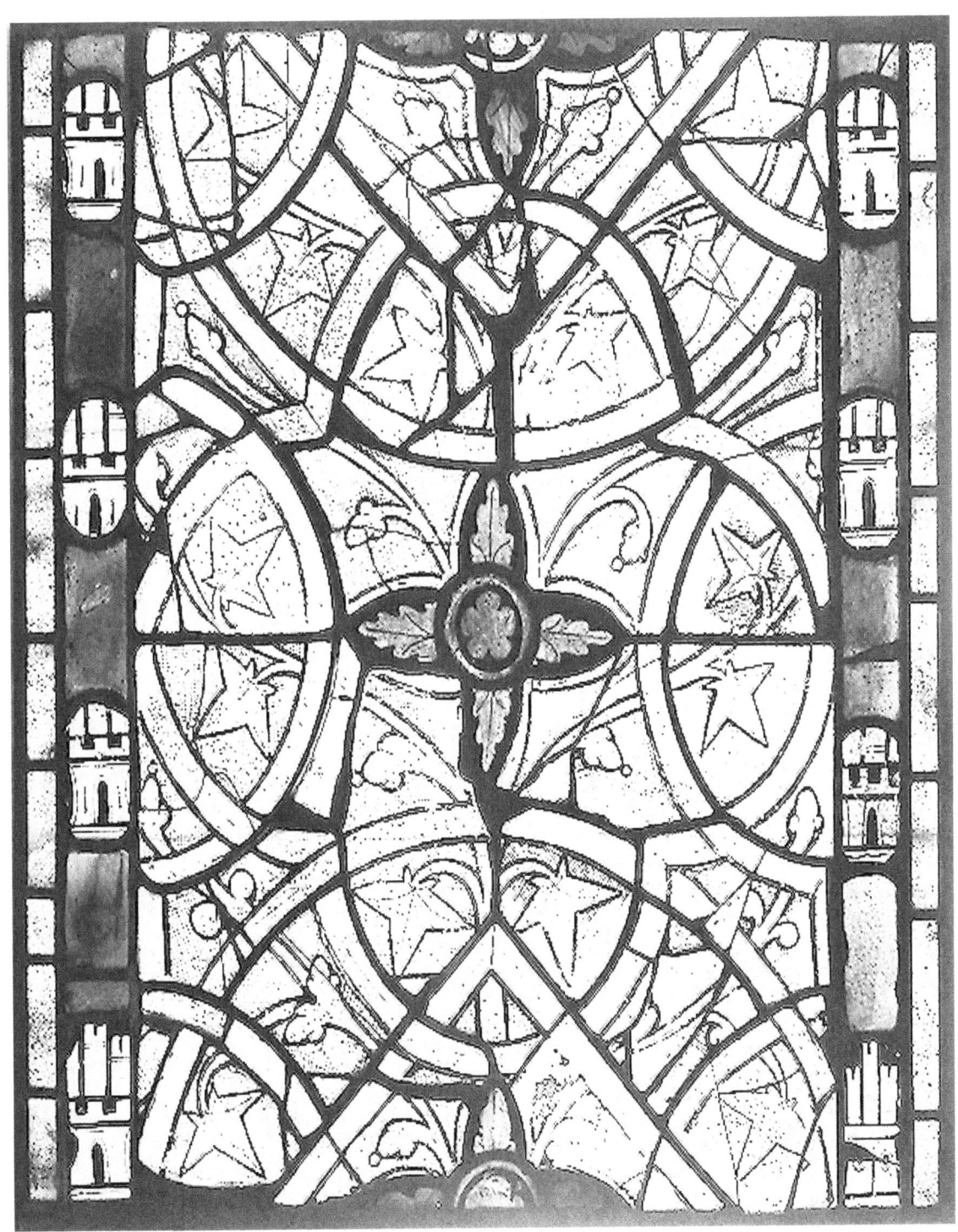

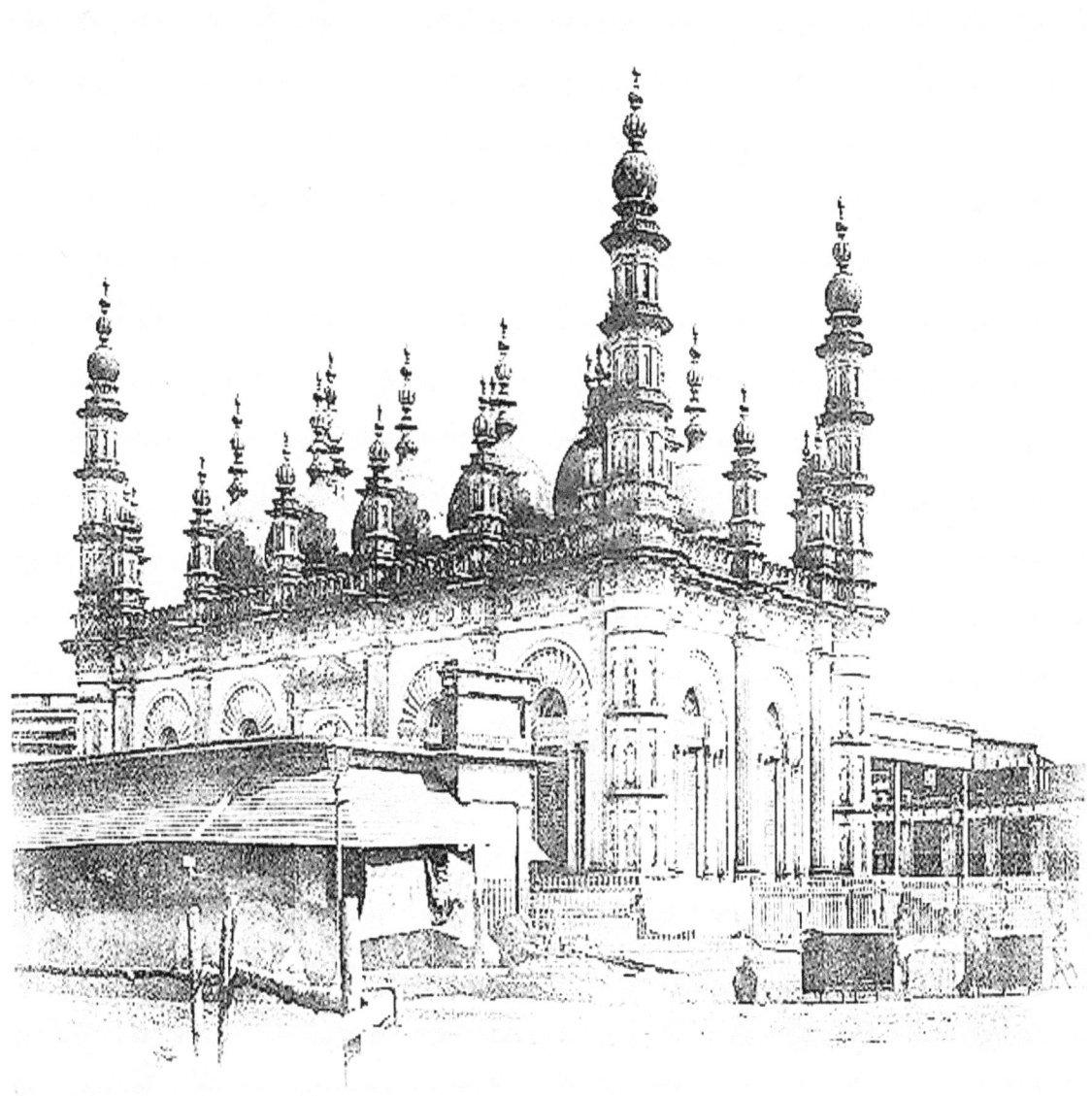

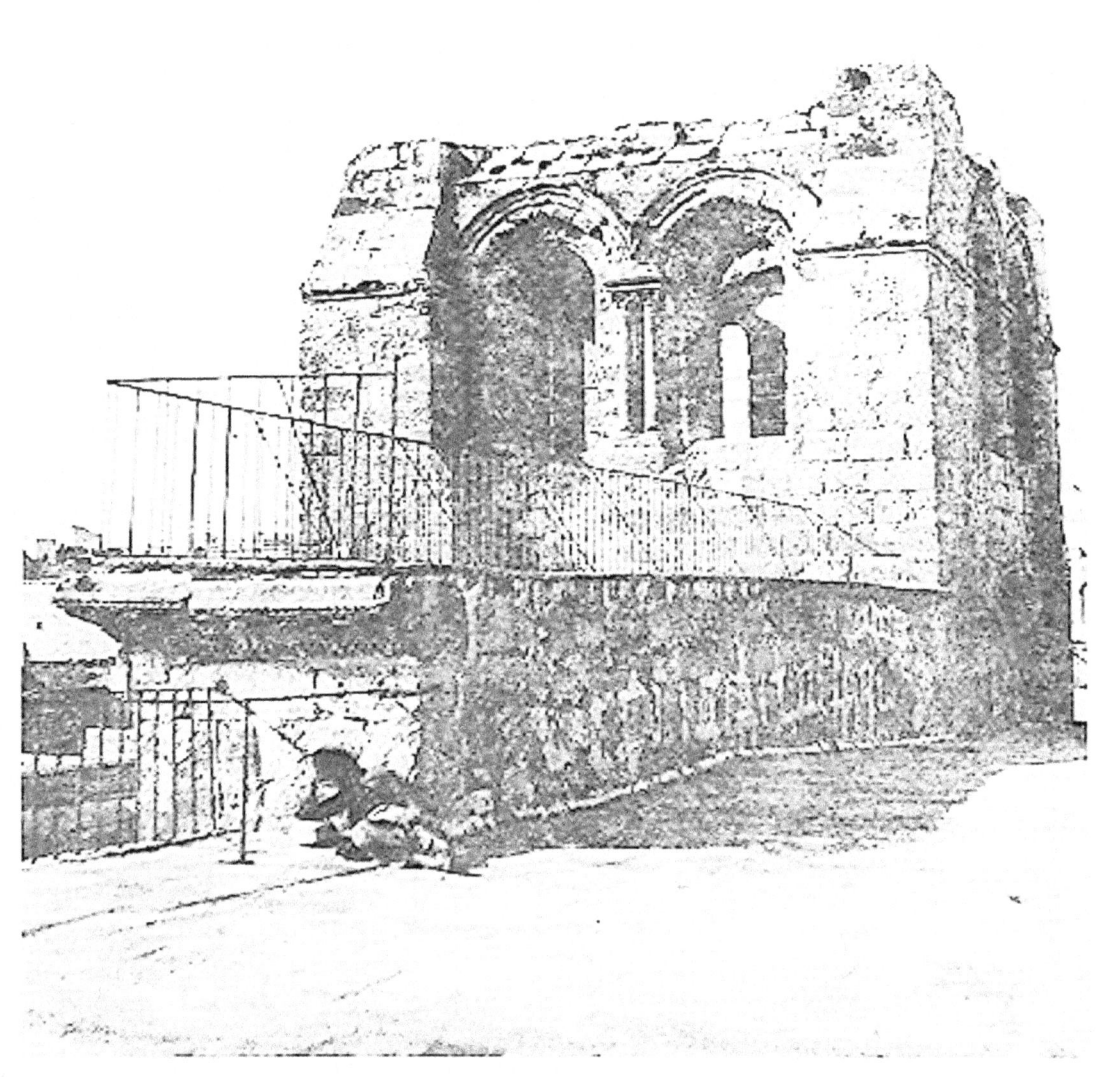

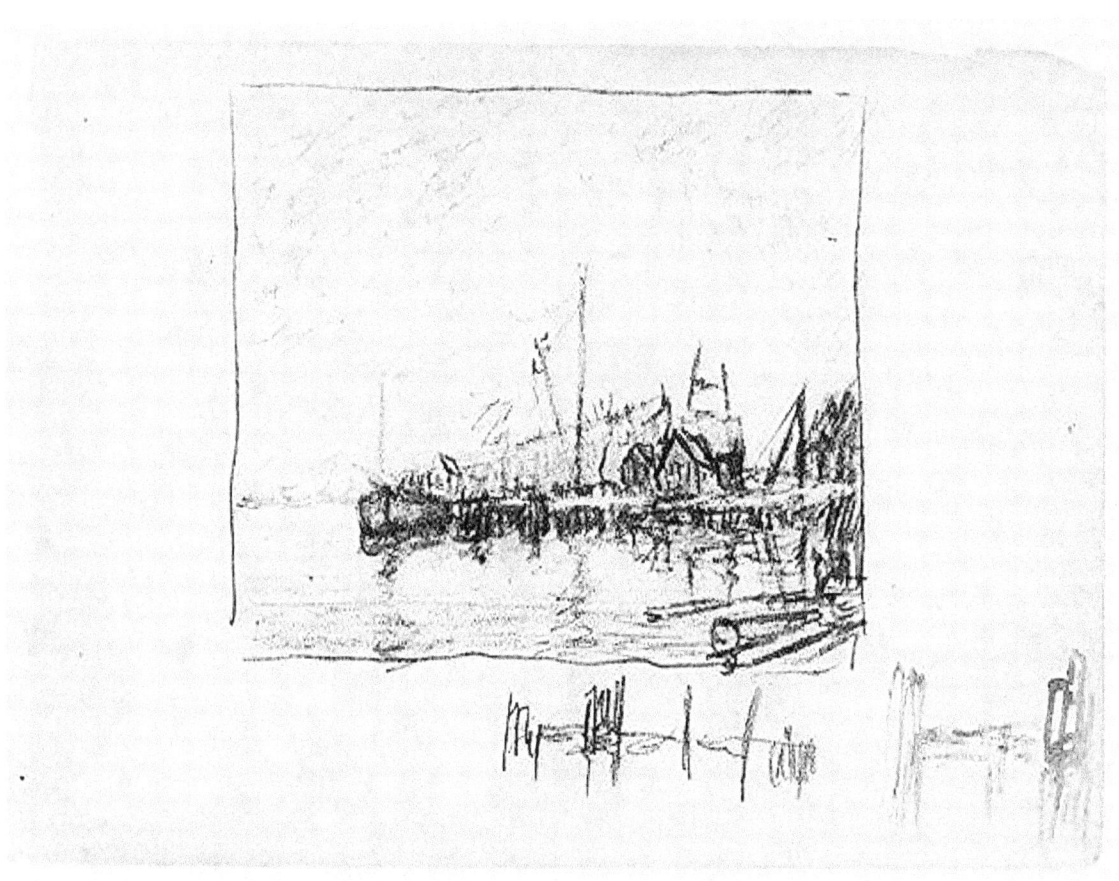

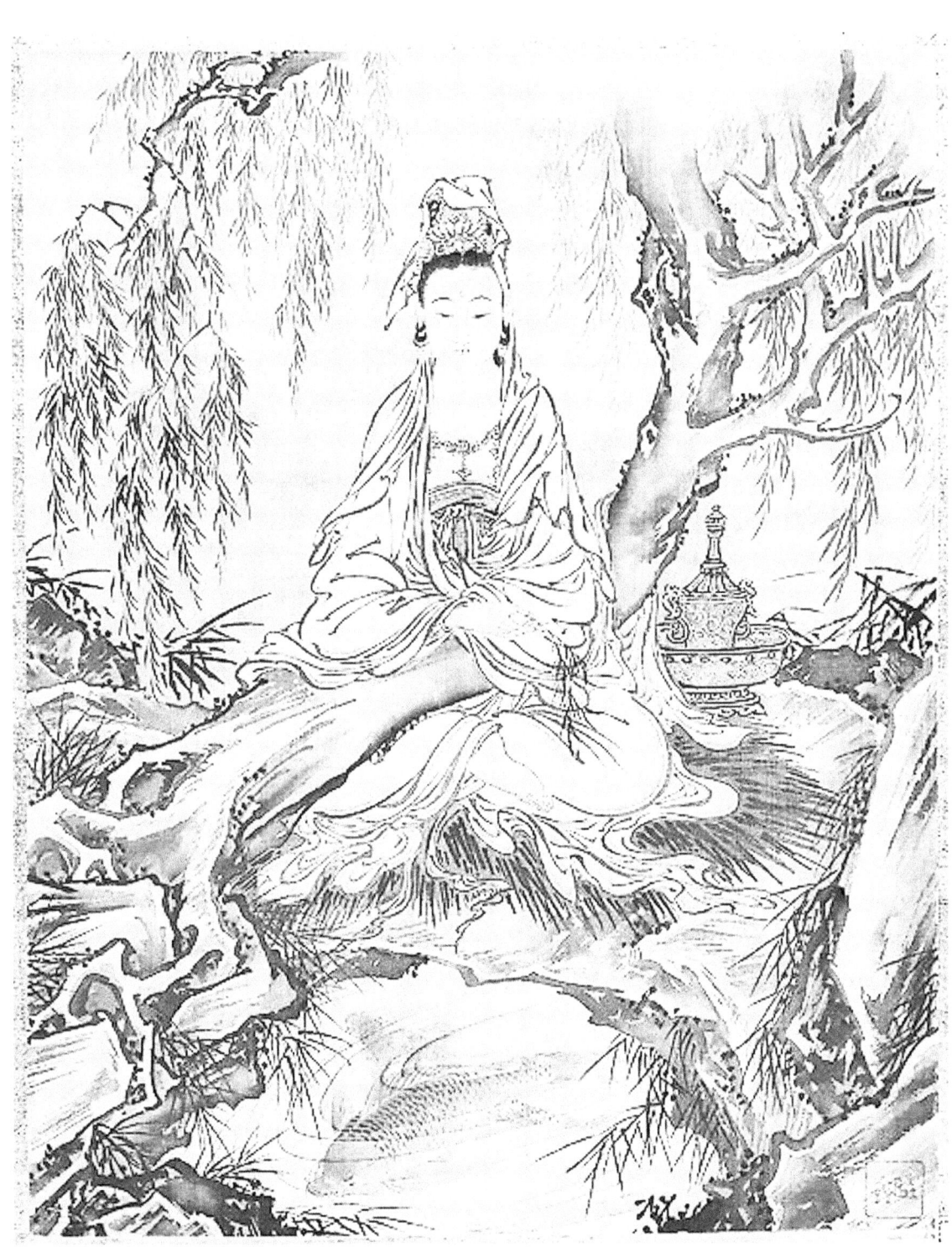

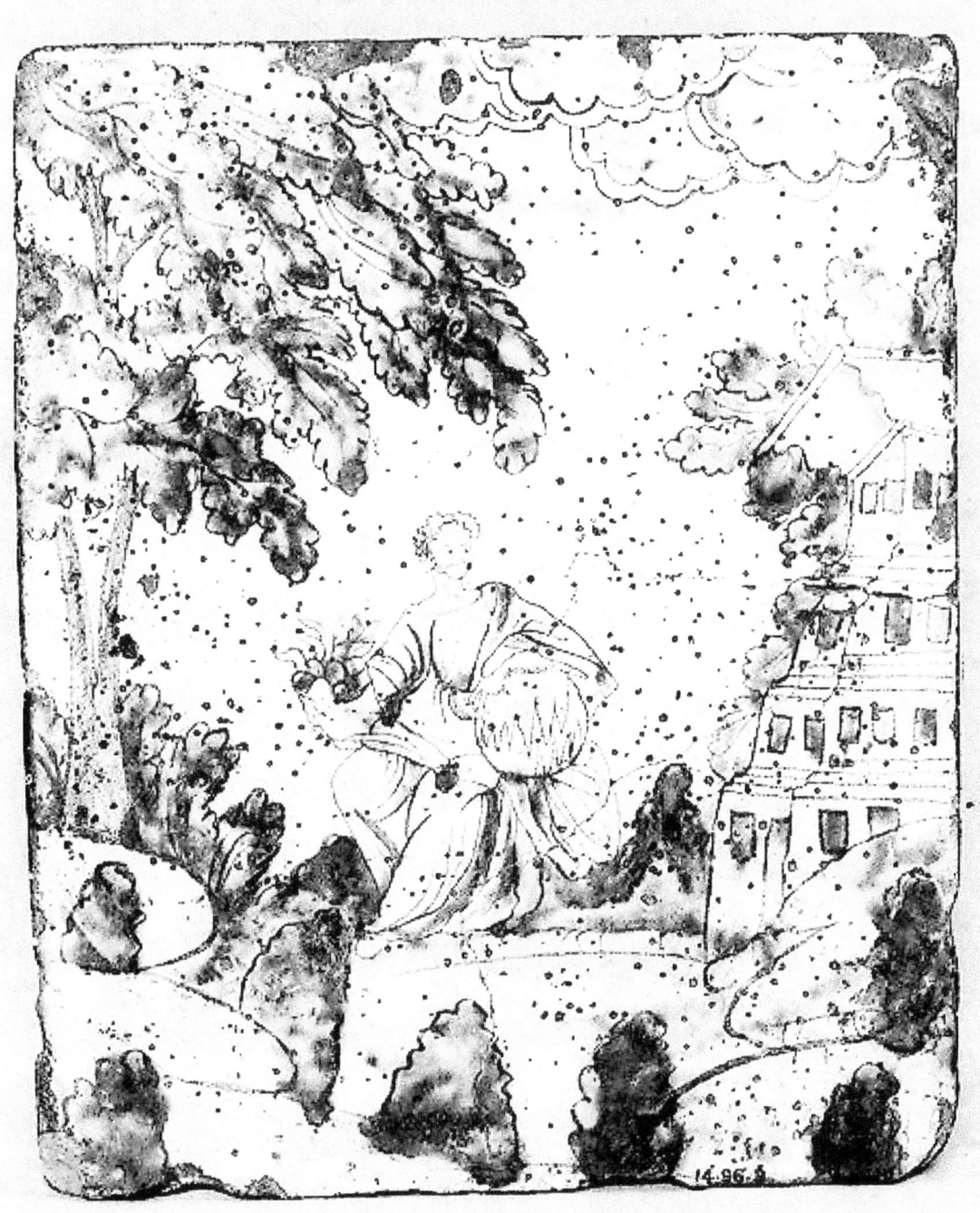

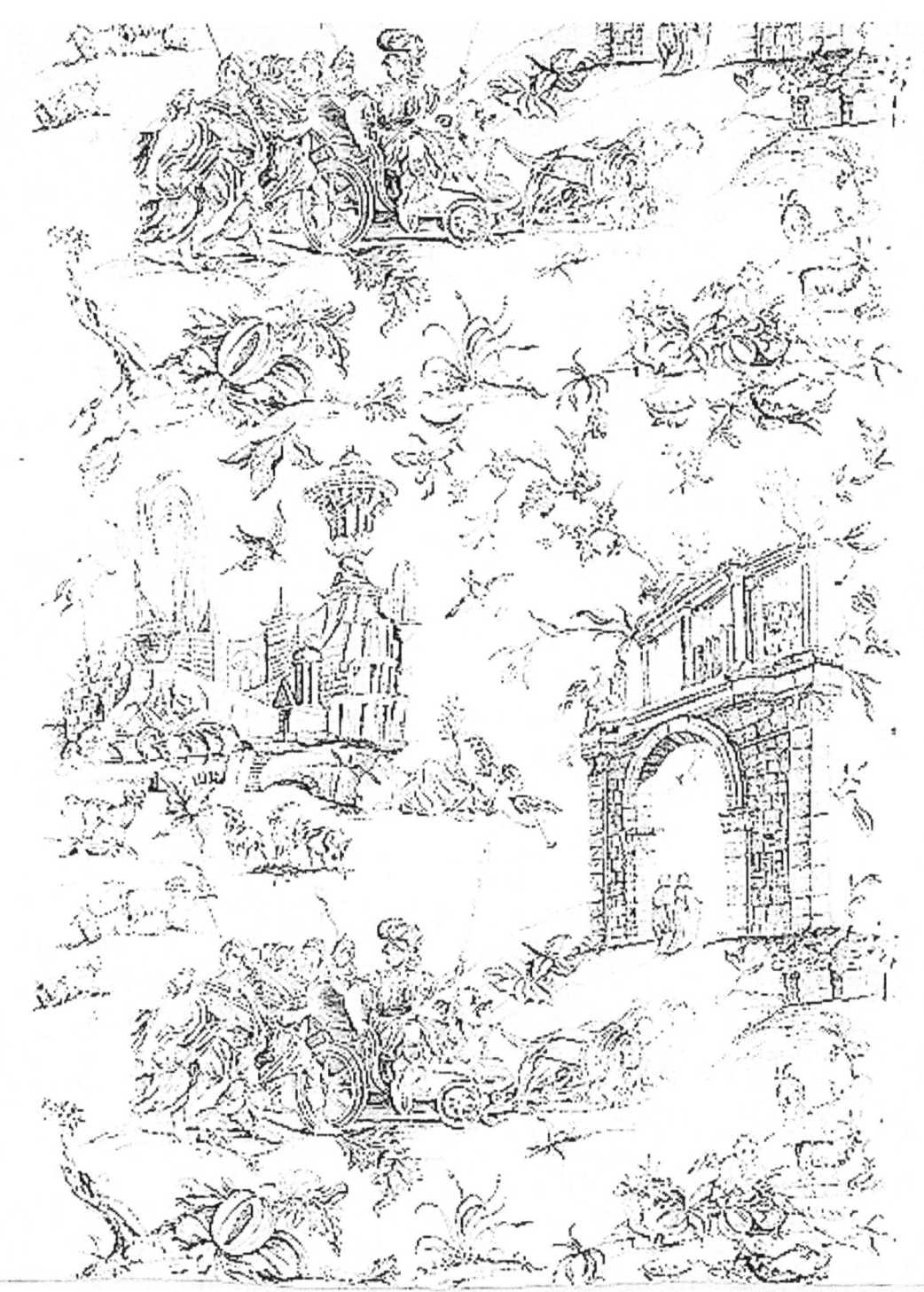

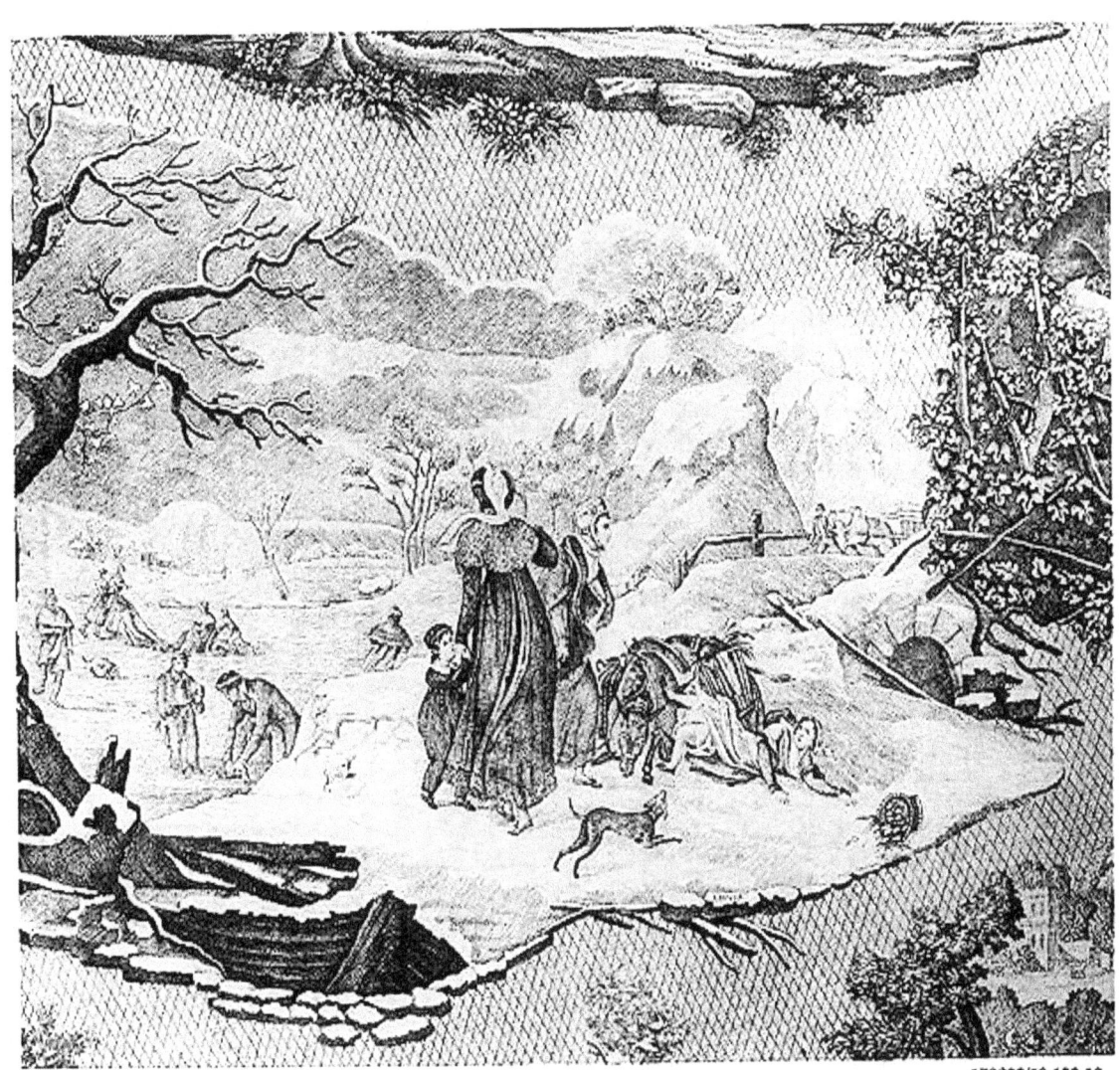

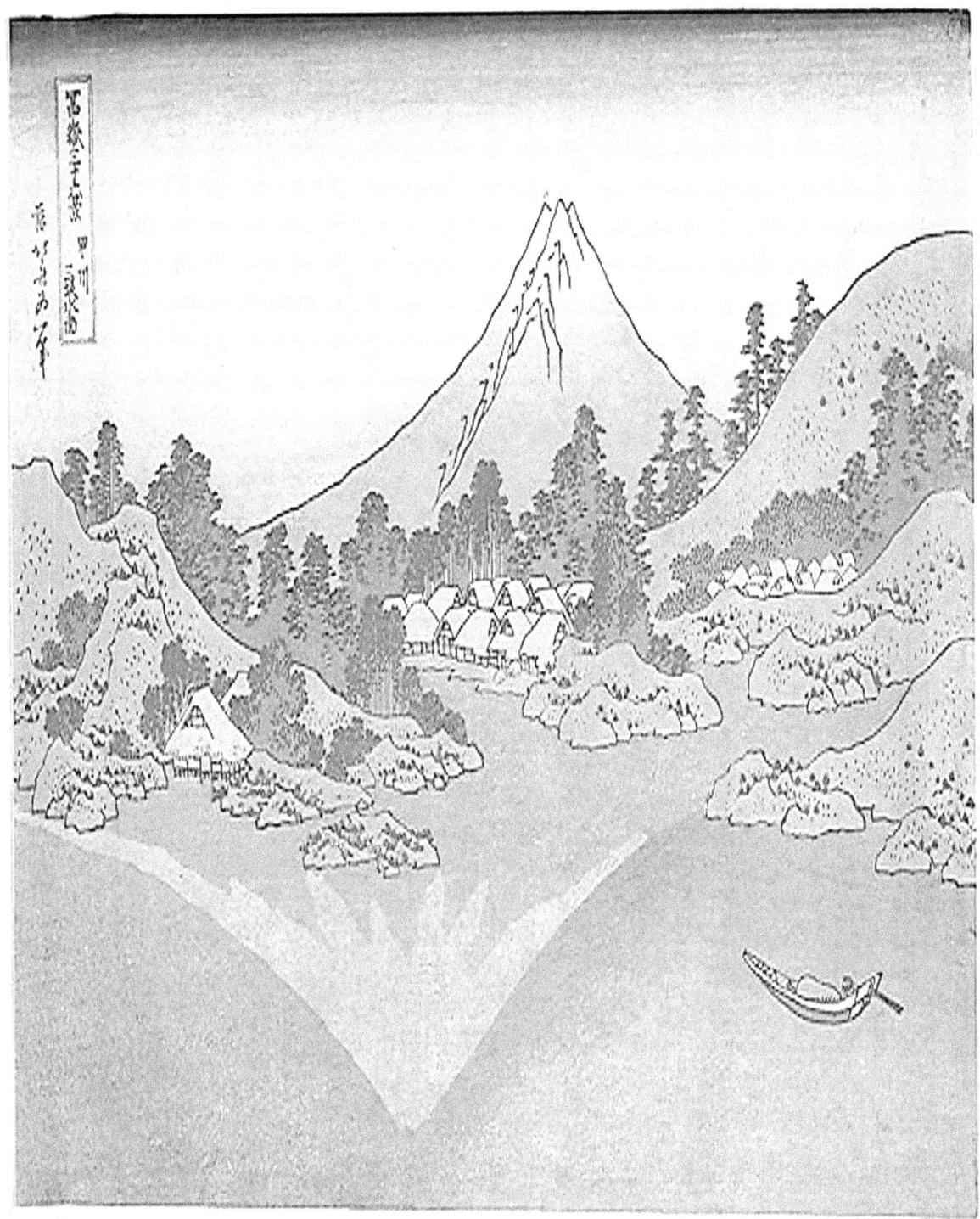

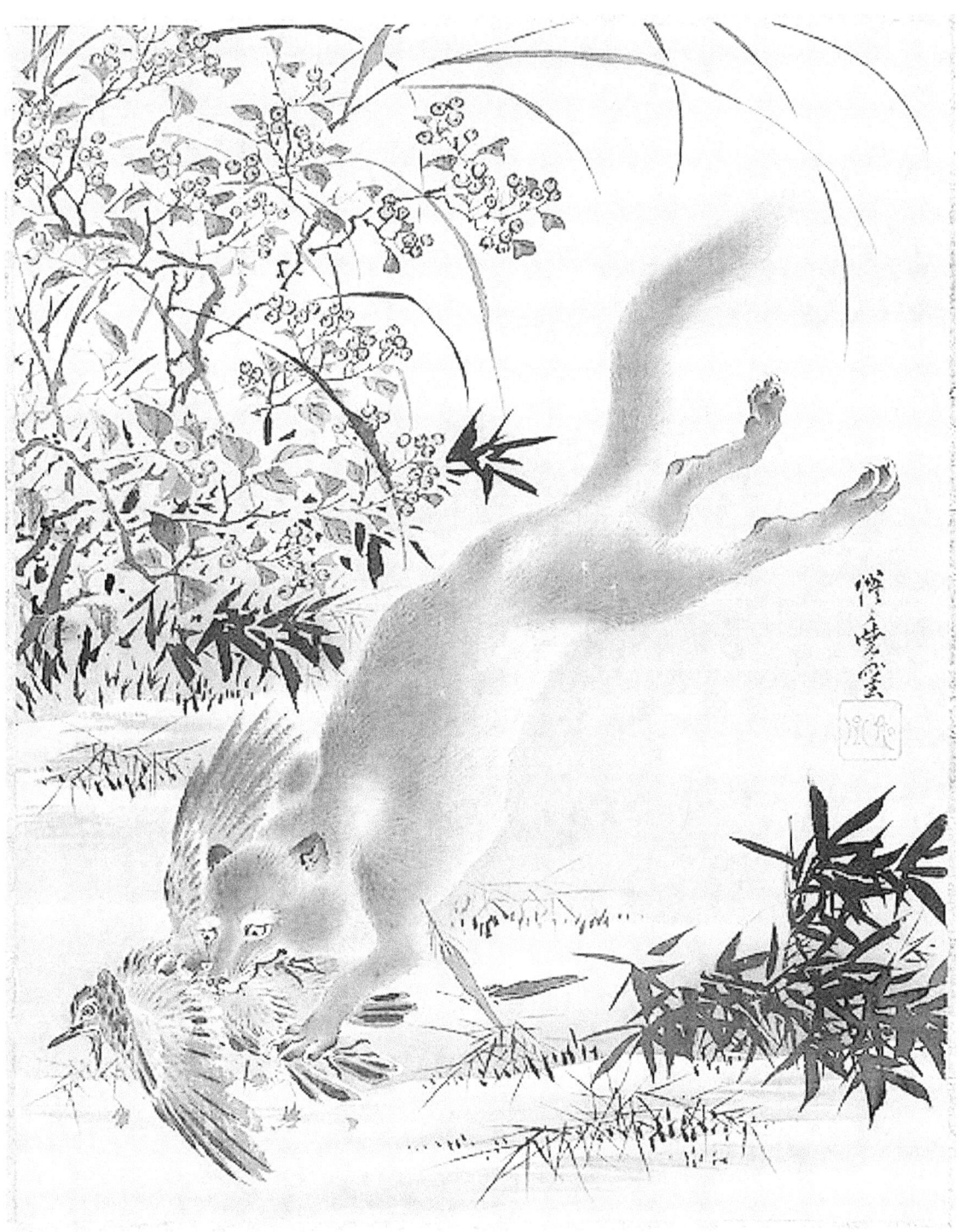

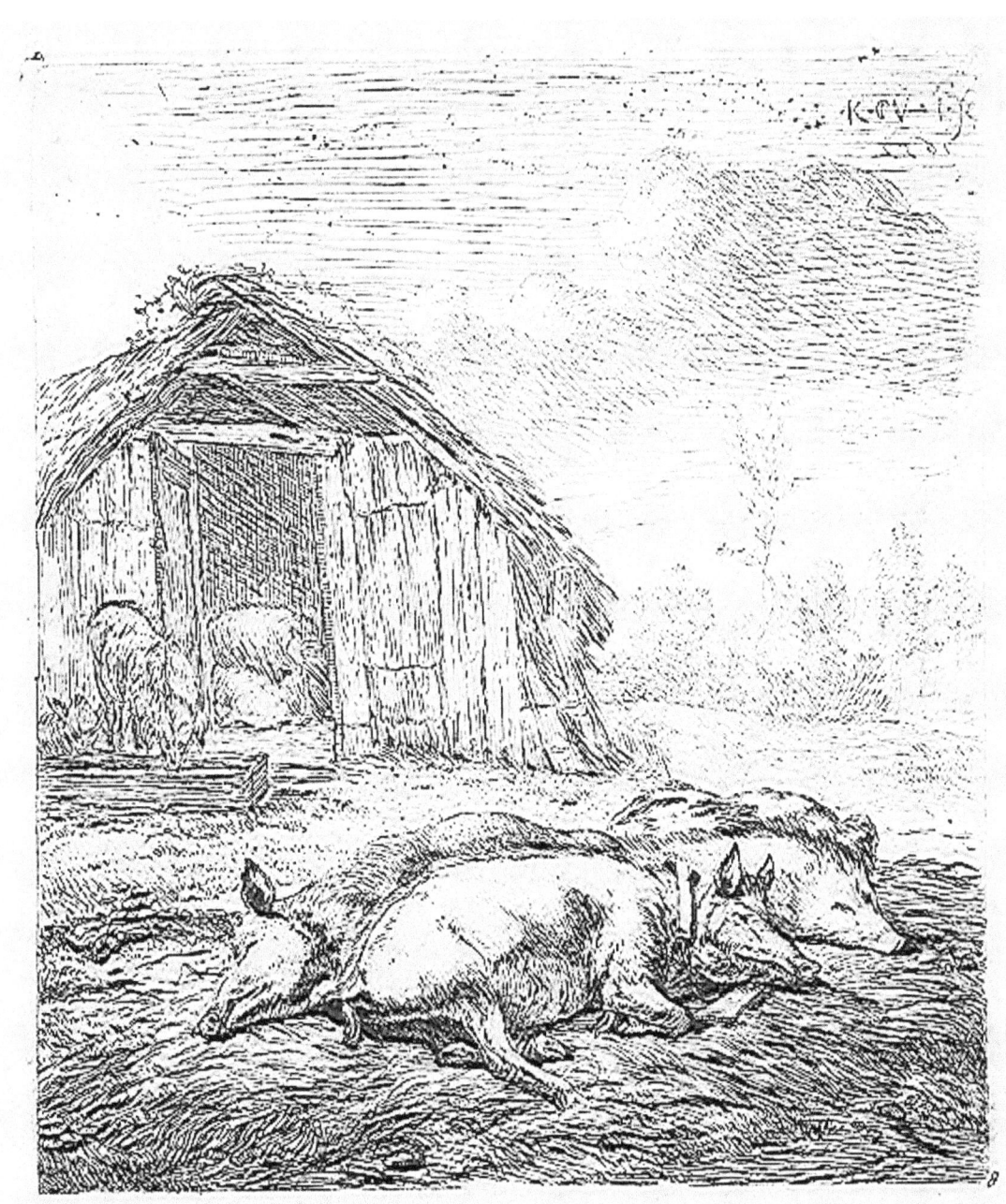

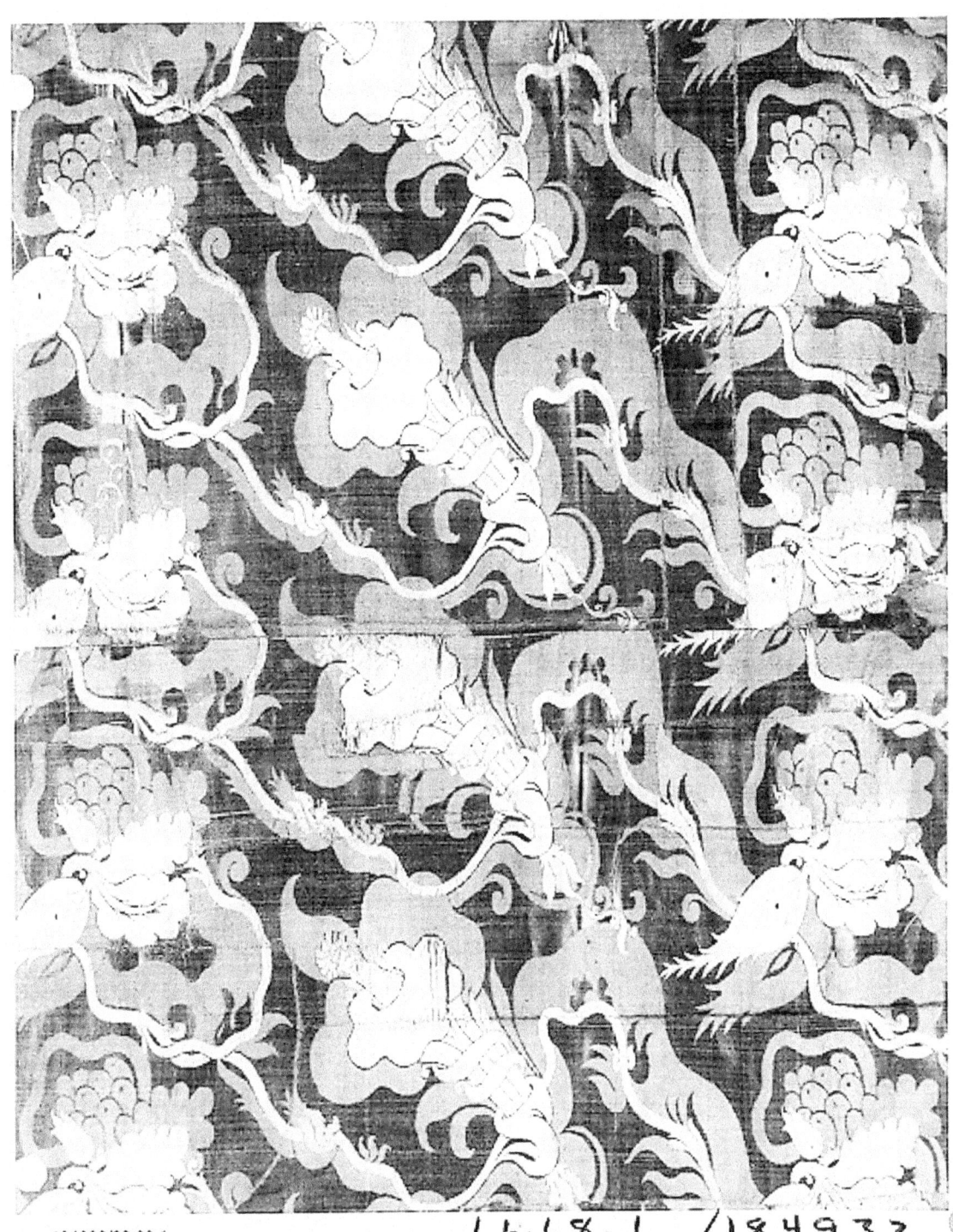

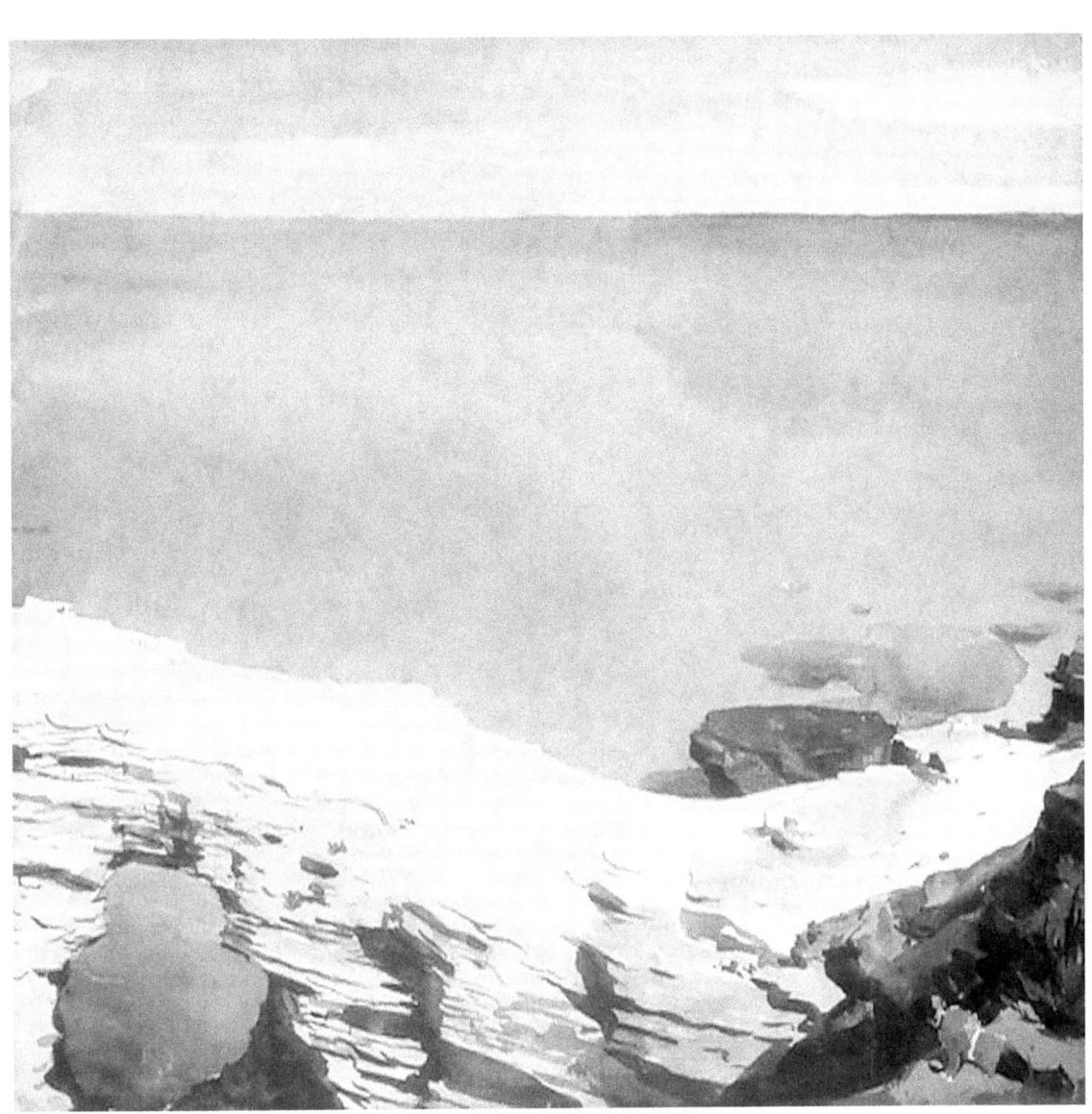

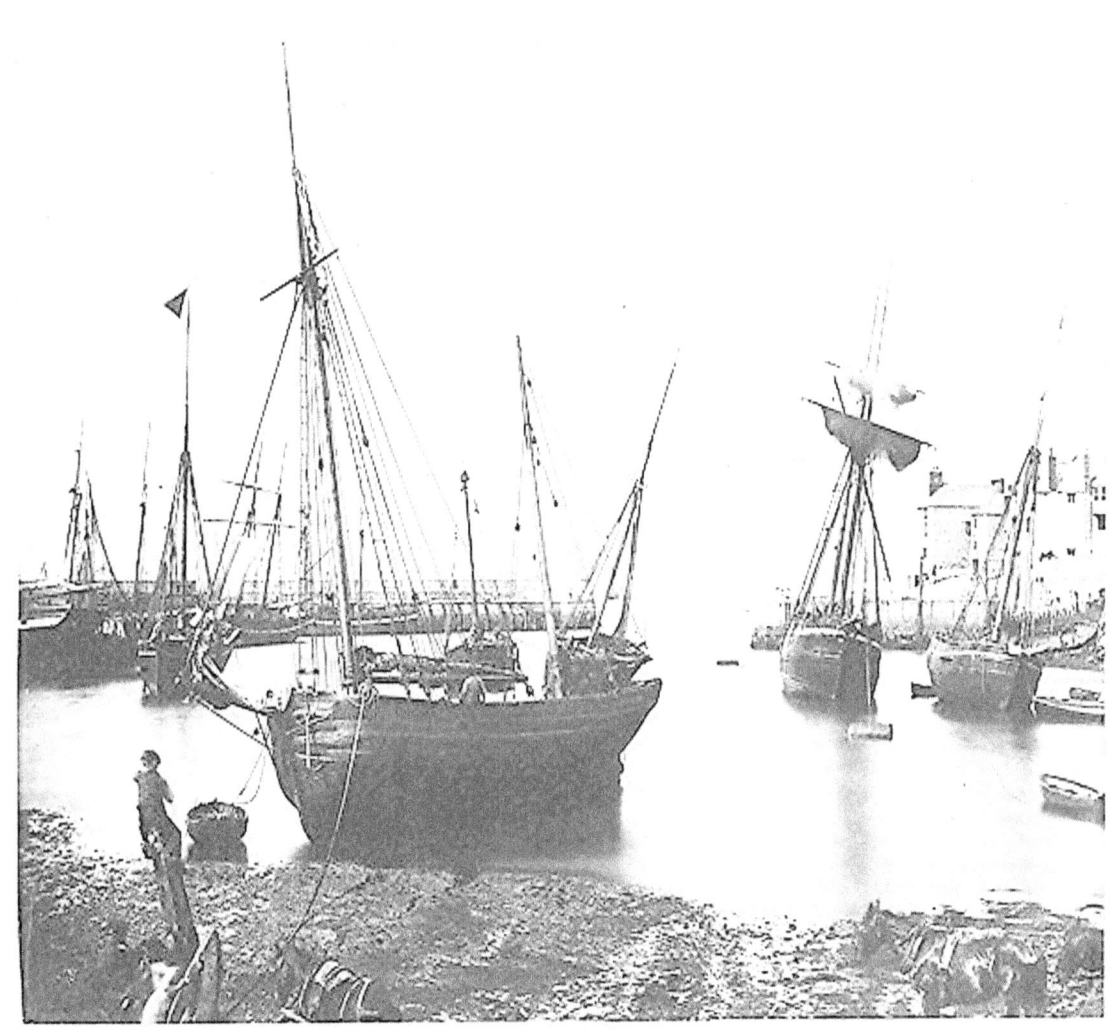

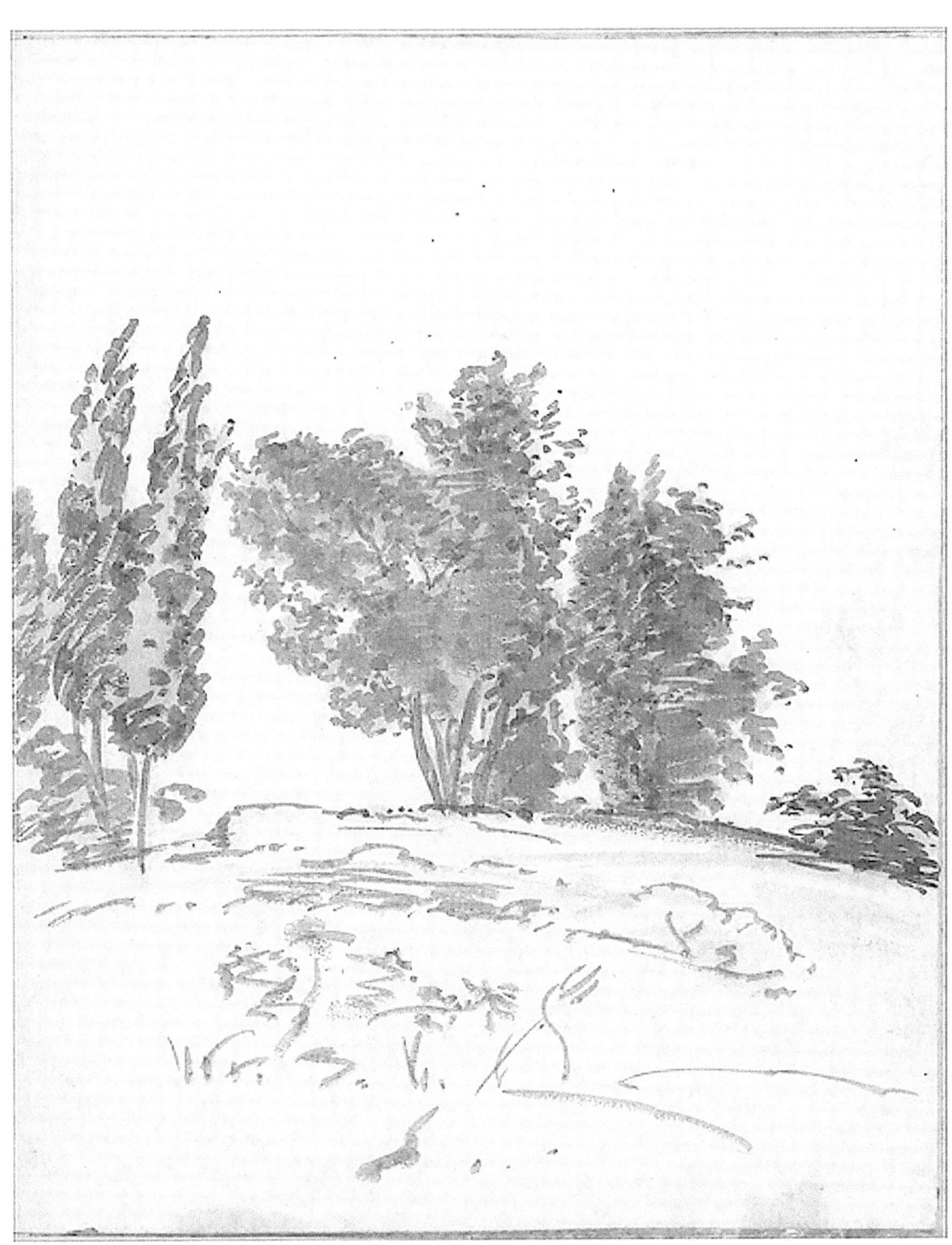

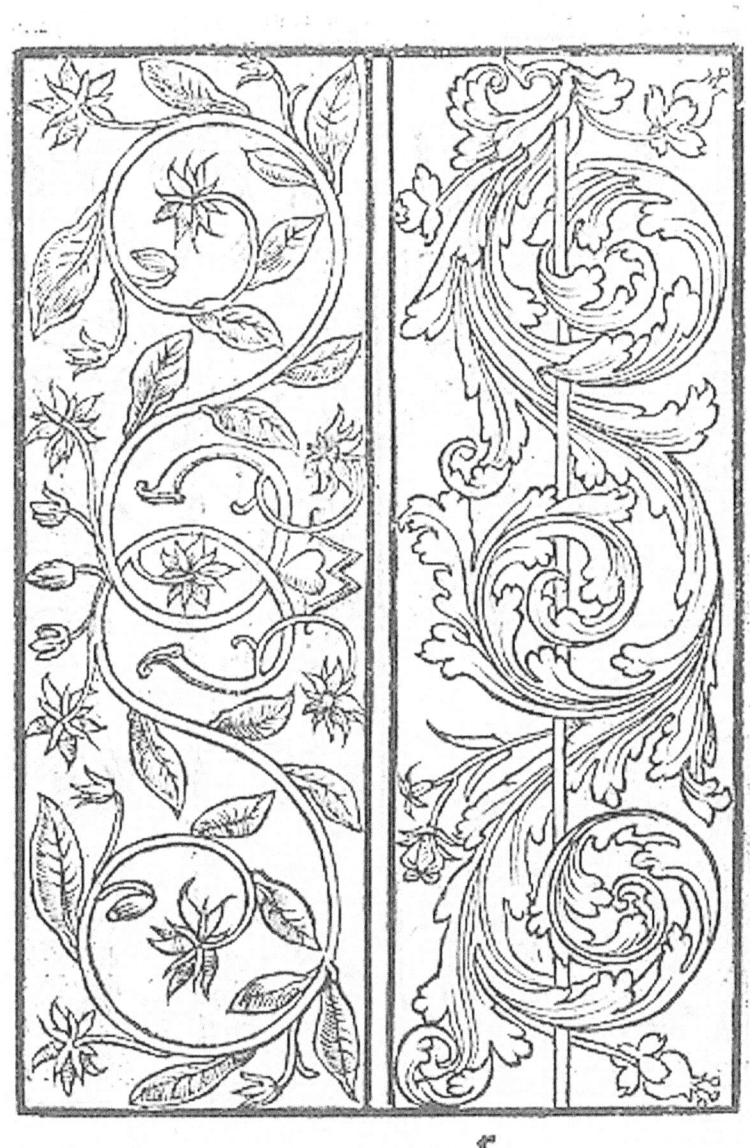

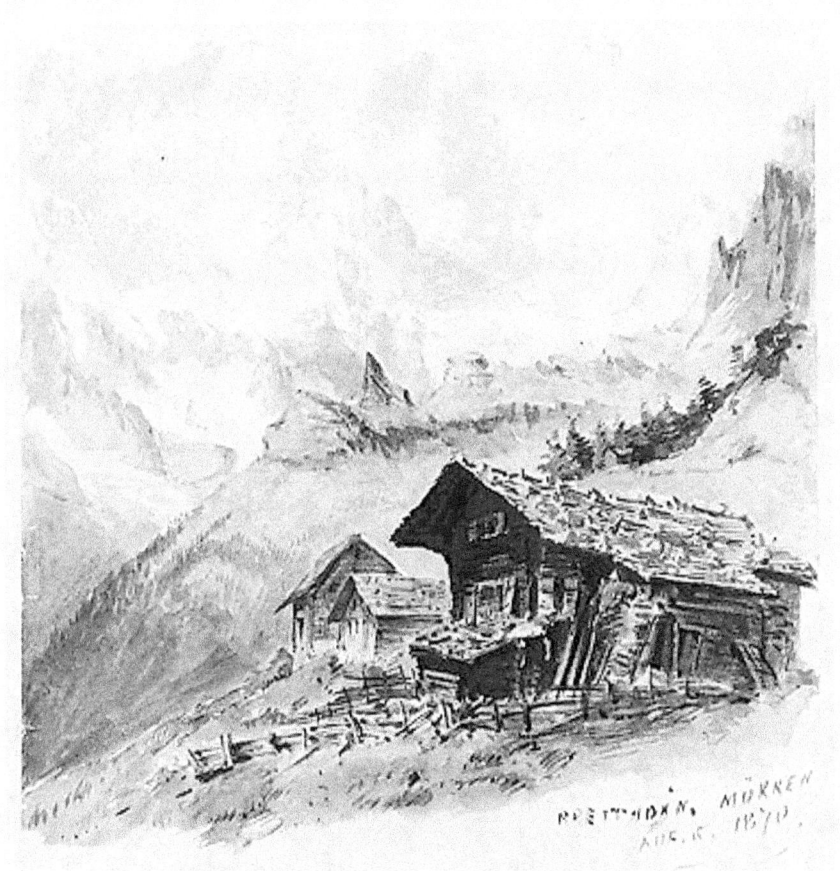

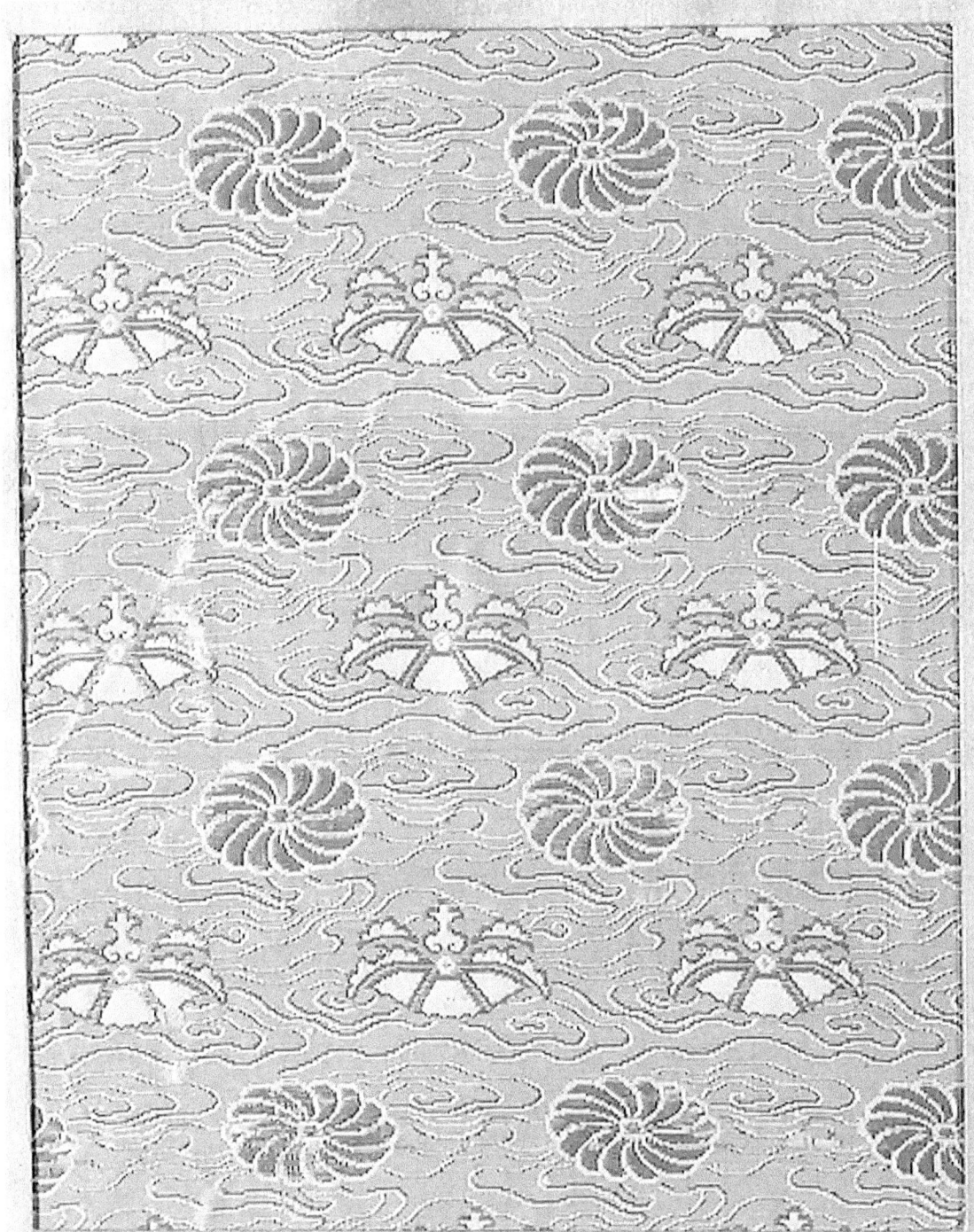

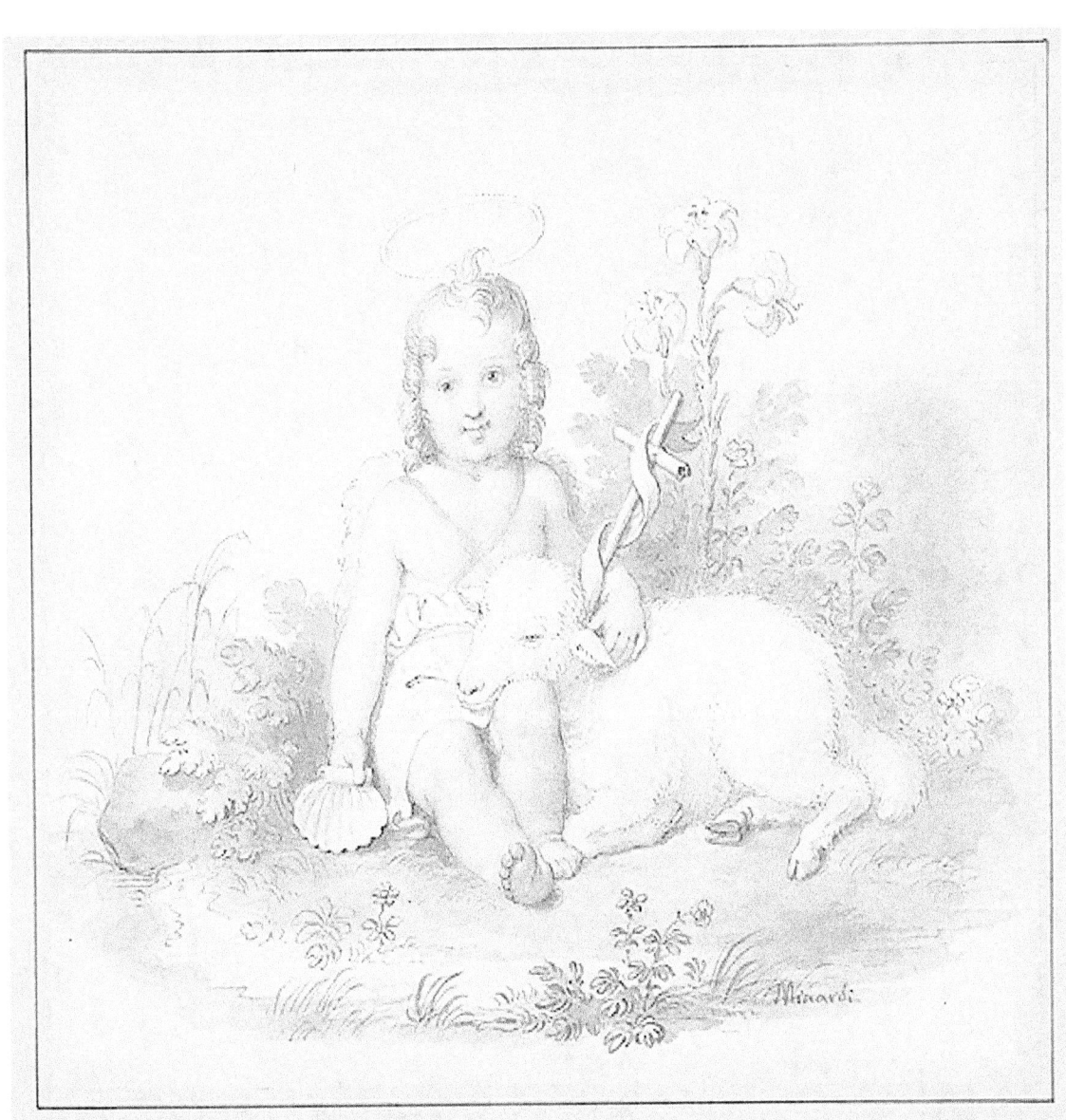

www.ingramcontent.com/pod-product-compliance
Lightning Source LLC
Chambersburg PA
CBHW062331220526
45469CB00008B/2665